MW01516973

Why the Tool?

Tools have been important to the success of the human race since the dawn of time. Unlike other species, humans are adept at building and using tools to accomplish specific and important tasks. In the modern era, software tools are the latest innovation in moving humanity forward in the tools frontier. Microsoft is proud to continue to innovate and provide new software tools and contribute to an improved society for all.

The Caliper

The caliper (sometimes also spelled calliper) is a measuring instrument that consists of two adjustable legs or jaws for measuring the dimensions of material parts. Caliper is derived from the word "calibre," meaning the diameter of a hole (as in a firearm) or of a cylindrical or spherical body. Outside calipers measure thicknesses and outside diameters of objects; inside calipers measure hole diameters and distances between surfaces. To check the dimensions of a machined part, the calipers are first adjusted to the required dimension on a ruler or a standard plug or hole gauge; accuracy in calipering depends in large part on the sense of touch of the operator. Calipers were known to both the Greeks and Romans, although uncommonly used. They were also known to be used during the Middle Ages for stonework and construction of cathedrals.

THE MICROSOFT®
.NET
FRAMEWORK

Microsoft®
.net™

Based on Beta Content

Microsoft®

PUBLISHED BY
Microsoft Press
A Division of Microsoft Corporation
One Microsoft Way
Redmond, Washington 98052-6399

Library of Congress Cataloging-in-Publication Data
The Microsoft .NET Framework / Microsoft Corporation.
      p. cm.
   Includes index.
   ISBN 0-7356-1444-X
   1. Microsoft.net framework.   2. Computer software--Standards.   3. Microsoft software.
  I. Microsoft Corporation.

  QA76.754 .M537 2001
  005.2'76--dc21   2001030479

Printed and bound in the United States of America.

1 2 3 4 5 6 7 8 9   QWE   6 5 4 3 2 1

Distributed in Canada by Penguin Books Canada Limited.

A CIP catalogue record for this book is available from the British Library.

Microsoft Press books are available through booksellers and distributors worldwide. For further information about international editions, contact your local Microsoft Corporation office or contact Microsoft Press International directly at fax (425) 936-7329. Visit our Web site at mspress.microsoft.com. Send comments to *mspinput@microsoft.com*.

Acquisitions Editor: Juliana Aldous
Project Editor: Denise Bankaitis

Body Part No. X08-19535

Contents

Preface

If you are holding this book in your hands, no doubt you want information about Microsoft .NET and you want it now. You have heard about how .NET will allow developers to create programs that will transcend device boundaries and fully harness the connectivity of the Internet in their applications. You have read in the news journals that Microsoft will soon be releasing a new programming language called C# that is derived from C and C++ and is part of Visual Studio.NET. You are curious about .NET, what Microsoft has planned, and how you can be a part of it.

This book contains some of the most requested topics on Microsoft .NET available through the Microsoft Developer Network (MSDN)—Microsoft's premier developer resource. *The Microsoft .NET Framework* is one book in a series that includes *Microsoft C# Language Specifications*, *The Microsoft .NET Framework Developer Specifications*, *Web Applications in the Microsoft .NET Framework*, and *Microsoft VisualStudio.NET*. Within this series, you'll find important technical articles from *MSDN Magazine* and MSDN Online as well as subject matter overviews and white papers from Microsoft and industry experts. You will also find transcripts of key speeches and interviews with top Microsoft product managers. We have also included the documentation and specifications for the new C# language and other key documents. And code…lots and lots of code.

Who Is This Book For?

This book is for developers who are interested in being on the cutting edge of new technologies and languages. It's for developers who are eager to learn, want to stay ahead of the curve, and aren't willing to wait until everything is in place and wrapped up in a pretty package. If you fit these criteria, order a pizza and settle in—this book is for you.

What's in This Book?

This book is a basic primer for the .NET Framework. While Microsoft .NET is the Microsoft strategy for delivering software as a service—the .NET Framework is the environment used for building those services. Consisting of the Common Language Runtime, the Framework classes, and ASP.NET, the .NET Framework is used for building, deploying, and running Web Services and other applications.

This book begins with the vision for the whole .NET platform as presented by Bill Gates during his keynote speech at Forum 2000. Once you read about and understand the vision of .NET, you can then find the answers to the basic .NET Framework questions in a straightforward FAQ. At this point, the book dives deep into the architecture of .NET and the .NET Framework through a series of interviews conducted by Robert Hess of MSDN .NET Show. Robert interviews key Microsoft architects and programmers including John Shewchuck, Mark Anders, Anders Hejlsberg and Brian Harry—the folks closest and most qualified to discuss .NET. From these experts, you'll learn how .NET affects the future of the Web, what issues programmers will face using the .NET Framework, how programmers can benefit from .NET, and how to use the .NET Framework class libraries. After reading the book, be sure to download the .NET Framework, which is available to the public at the MSDN website, and test it for yourself.

A Warning

Microsoft is offering this material as a first look, but remember that it's not final. Be sure to read any warnings posted on MSDN before installing any beta products. Visit MSDN regularly, and check for updates and the latest information.

About MSDN

MSDN makes it easy to find timely, comprehensive development resources and stay current on development trends and Microsoft technology. MSDN helps you keep in touch with the development community, giving you opportunities to share information and ideas with your peers and communicate directly with Microsoft. Check out the many resources of MSDN.

MSDN Online

More than just technical articles and documentation, MSDN Online (http://msdn.microsoft.com) is *the* place to go when looking for Microsoft developer resources. On MSDN Online, you can

- Search the MSDN Library and Knowledge Base for technical documentation
- Visit an online Developer Center for resource listings on popular topics
- View and download sample applications and code, or make and review comments through the Code Center
- Participate in peer developer forums such as Newsgroups, Peer Journal, Members Helping Members, and Ratings & Comments
- Find technical seminars, trade shows, and conferences sponsored or supported by Microsoft, and then easily register online

MSDN Publications

MSDN Publications (http://msdn.microsoft.com/magazines) offers print and online publications for current information on all types of development. The following is a list of just a few of the publications MSDN produces.

- *MSDN Magazine*—a monthly magazine featuring real-world solutions built with Microsoft technologies, as well as early looks at upcoming products and new directions, such as Microsoft .NET
- *The .NET Show* (MSDN Show)—a regular series of webcasts about Microsoft's hottest technologies
- *MSDN Online Voices*—an online collection of regular technical columns updated each week
- *MSDN News*—a bimonthly newspaper of technical articles and columns for MSDN subscribers

MSDN Subscriptions

With an MSDN subscription (http://msdn.microsoft.com/subscriptions), you can get your hands on essential Microsoft developer tools, Microsoft .NET Servers, Visual Studio.NET, and Microsoft operating systems. Available on CD and DVD, as well as online through MSDN Subscriber downloads, an MSDN subscription also provides you with

- Monthly shipments of the latest Microsoft Visual Studio development system, Microsoft .NET Enterprise Servers, Microsoft operating systems, and Visio 2000
- The latest updates, SDKs, DDKs, and essential programming information

Forum 2000 Keynote: Bill Gates Speaks About the .NET Platform

During his keynote speech at Forum 2000, Microsoft Corporation Chairman and Chief Software Architect Bill Gates talks about the next-generation platform called .NET. A transcript of the speech is available at the Microsoft.com Web site. Microsoft's efforts going forward will be focused on the .NET platform. The .NET platform will affect every piece of application code that is written and will redefine the user interface as much as the transition from MS-DOS to Windows did. It will make it possible to get information anytime and anywhere, using a natural interface. A new generation of full-screen and small-screen devices will be available to the user. The world of programming will also change, with XML being the base protocol for this new era. In the coming years, Microsoft will continue to channel resources toward this exciting new platform.

Bill Gates: Well, it's exciting to finally be here and have a chance to talk about this next generation of software that we're building. We had a meeting a couple months ago where we sat down and said, "Okay, what is it that we really want to explain here?" And when I walked into the meeting they had a slide up that said, "We have to explain CSA." And I sat down and I thought, "What does CSA stand for?" And I thought, "Well, I'll just play along here. It should become clear. You know, I understand what's going on around here."

And so they were talking and talking and, you know, it wasn't clear at all. So I thought, "Well, I guess I'll have to make a fool of myself and ask what CSA is, because it's clearly this thing we have to explain at this event, so I'd better know what it is." Well, it turns out that CSA stands for Chief Software Architect. *(Laughter.)* And so in a little bit I get to explain how I've spent the last six months since I've been Chief Software Architect, and with the shipment of Windows 2000 we really have this opportunity to focus our efforts in a new direction and conquer some new horizons.

A lot of what you're going to hear about today are things that we've been working towards for a long time. I'd even go back to vision efforts like the Information At Your Fingertips work that we did back in 1990. There's a big difference between what we're talking about today and that vision. The difference is that the underlying technology and the ability to actually make all of those things concrete is now quite clear—quite clear because of the industry progress over the last few years, quite clear because of the investments we've made in basic research over the intervening years. And so what we're going to be talking about today is something that is very concrete for us, even though it rolls out over a many year period.

First, let me start by talking about how we see the industry framework, what's really going on.

Well, we're certainly moving to a digital world. You know, we can see this progress month by month. You know, photos with these great digital cameras, the ability to touch them up, put them in an album, send them around; still a lot to do before that's 100 percent for the way that photos are done, but we're getting there.

Music: the ability to have small devices that contain literally hundreds or thousands of your songs, where you can sequence them the way you want to. In fact, the main issue about digital music is making sure that people are willing to pay for it, as well as being able to use it.

Video editing has been a tough challenge, because of the size and the speed of the processor required for that application. But with the next version of Windows we include that application and you're starting to see great digital cameras.

Note taking is probably one that surprises you to see on the list there. That's something we'll be talking about a fair bit today. We've always believed that you should have a digital device, a full-screen device with you wherever you go, so even in an event like this one it's our view that you'd have a full-screen digital device, where you're fully connected and your notes are recognized and searchable, just like all the other material you work with.

In the world of business we talk about how transactions are done over the Internet, but if you really dig into that and say, "Okay, what happens if the product's going to be late? What happens if you receive what shipped and it actually doesn't meet the specifications?" Today, that kind of complex business dialogue is not done on a digital basis. It's only the most straightforward transaction that goes on there.

And so the idea of taking buying and selling and really matching up every buyer with every seller and taking the richness of that relationship, including the customer service and the unexpected events and bringing digital efficiency to that; that's still a horizon that has not been conquered.

The final point here is thinking about knowledge workers. Their world today is very bifurcated. Yes, the PC has been a wonderful thing in terms of document creation, PowerPoint presentations and spreadsheets, but as they work through their day there's a lot of paperwork, there's a lot of handwritten notes, there's a lot of meetings that, you know, are purely analog. They can't go back and take a snippet of that meeting, send it around. They can't search the meeting to see what happened. If they want to go to a meeting and learn something, they can't test their knowledge in a digital fashion.

So we have an opportunity to take this vision of a digital world and apply the magic of software to make this a reality.

But it's not quite like the past where there will be a single device that defines all of this. There will be many different devices. We'll talk today about the relative role of the small-screen devices and the full-screen devices, but I think you'll agree there's a substantial role for both of those, and even some variety within each of those categories.

And so the question of how do you take software to enable across many devices, that's a challenge we've been thinking about for the last few years.

Well, the Internet is the starting point here. The fact that it's at critical mass in terms of not only having Web sites, but doing business across those Web sites is very exciting. And that is truly a global phenomenon. The simplicity of pointing your browser at a URL, the simplicity of following a link, having a history list, that's a fantastic thing. And so the Internet is very, very much in the mainstream.

But what is it today? Well, primarily it's being able to connect up your screen to the presentation material on any different Web site. And so in a certain technical sense it's a lot like taking a 3270 terminal on a network and simply being able to connect up to many mainframes.

What you see is one site at a time. And that site has to be authored to your particular device, the kind of screen size that you've got, the kind of interaction techniques that are available there, the resolution. And so we're connecting things together, but we're not using the intelligence at either end, and we're not creating something that takes information from multiple sites.

When you get that page of information today it's basically read-only. In fact, imagine yourself trying to do a product forecast or even saying you want to buy from many potential sellers. You have to manually go to those different sites and either try and cut and paste the information, which doesn't work very well, or simply write it down on a piece of paper. And then you move from that world into your productivity applications, like Microsoft Office and you recreate the information there. And that's where you're able to compare the data, look at it graphically, and combine it with your own thinking about it. But that is a different world. That is not the world of the browser.

So we've got an environment that's read-only. It's an environment where the user isn't very much in control: the idea that somebody can send you junk mail at any time or when you're sitting and working on something mail that's fairly low priority will come in and grab your attention. All the different things that are going on in the Internet, if you want to see if something changed, that's basically a manual process that you're spending your time trying to find those things out.

There are many islands in this world. If you take your PC at home, your PC at work, it's a manual operation to try and move your favorites, move your files or any of the other things around between those. If you have a PDA type device, you have to go through the effort of deciding what subset of the information you want to download. When you're connected up over a low-speed link, it's very complex to control which e-mail or other files or notifications come down onto your device.

So it's up to the user to manage these islands. And when you get into issues like group naming and security across these various islands, it's clear that the infrastructure is simply not rich enough.

Finally, this is an Internet where the keyboard is our primary means of interaction. We're still typing in commands. Over the last few decades I'm sure you've all seen lots and lots of demos of handwriting, speech recognition, visual type inferences with a camera, but the question has always been when is somebody going to build that into a system and create a programming model so that all the applications—and when I say applications I include all Web sites in that. It's a broad definition. When is somebody going to define it so those things can declare what sort of language, what sort of verbs or actions they're capable of?

So you need a programming model for this natural interface. And having the tools that let you do that and having the rich system, that's really the starting point for getting away from the keyboard being the only way that we interact.

So in the world where we go beyond browsing you can think of the Internet as more than a presentation network. It truly becomes a full platform, where you have intelligence on servers, intelligence on clients, working on behalf of the user.

Now what does that mean? That means that when you want to see information, if you're planning a new product, your device can go out to many different Web sites and extract exactly the information that's interesting to you. And if we do it right, it can bring it into the view that you're using to do your creativity, so that it's not just a read only screen you've got there, it is the full power of the device allowing you to do your work.

When we think about knowledge workers, they're not paid simply to click through screens and read what's there; their value added is taking that information and synthesizing it. And so by bringing those two worlds together, the world of reading, writing and annotation, we can allow them to do their job in a different way.

Now, when we think about multiple sites and customizing the information and combining it in the right way, obviously we're using a protocol that goes beyond HTML. HTML is defined purely for presentation. As you're going to hear today, XML is the base protocol for this new era. It is the thing that will be exchanged between sites, between sites and clients in order to build up these new capabilities.

We are saying that the natural interface richness will be built into this platform, and that's really putting a stake in the ground, because we're going to go out to developers and say, "Here's how you write your applications, so that handwriting and speech can interact naturally with that application."

We're also saying that the islands that we've got out there, certainly those can be broken down. The way to break it down is by putting out services that work across all the different devices, moving the information around, keeping track of which information is important and working on behalf of the user.

So that's the new concept, the concept of something running out in the Internet, out in the clouds, working on your behalf.

Well, XML is something that actually grew out of a document format called SGML, but it's really transformed itself into an essential way of exchanging heterogeneous data. And I'm not saying that the work around XML is done. In fact, you might say that it's just at the beginning, because for every real world object, whether it's a healthcare record, a banking record, a supply chain dialogue, around every one of those things we need rich standards. And we need very rich software tools that can map between different schemas, data layouts, map between one version of a schema and another version of a schema. So the very platform itself has to embrace XML in a very deep way.

It's exciting the progress that's taking place around XML just even in the last six months. We've got here a standard that Microsoft is very much behind, but not just Microsoft. We've got IBM and many others joining in things like the SOAP definition that explain how XML can essentially be used as a program to program protocol, how programs can exchange arbitrary data with each other.

And that's why we talk about the Web as a platform. You know, using XML, the idea that you go to many different sites and pull that information together using the intelligence of the device that becomes a reality.

And so it's really around those rich scenarios that all this work on XML is going on.

XML will transform productivity tools. For example, the spreadsheet will be changed by XML. The database will be changed by XML. The programming languages themselves will be changed. In fact, there will be language innovation in every popular programming language around XML. So it's a very profound change, even more profound than the change HTML brought to the world of presentation.

So what is Microsoft doing to help move this new world forward? One of the other questions that we had up in that meeting where they asked me to explain what CSA was, was that I had to explain why we spend billions and billions of dollars on R&D, and what was it, what were the big things that we're coming out about.

Well, this idea that we need a new platform, a platform that takes as its center the Internet and the user and then takes the devices and services those rather than having the devices at the center; that idea's been emerging for a long time. And the question is what can be done to get enough of those pieces together to really get that to critical mass.

Well, Microsoft is announcing today that our efforts as a company are going to be focused around this next generation platform. We call it .NET. That's a term you'll hear a lot today, and it encompasses more than one thinks. It encompasses the idea of putting rich code onto every one of these clients. It encompasses the idea of having services across the Internet that help every one of these clients. And then there's a new generation of servers that can work together providing those services that can either run inside of corporations, can run inside an ASP or can be run by the software creators themselves in order to allow all the users to get at that service capability.

There are some breakthrough elements that are necessary for this world. The user interface, which we're talking about now, as the user experience, will be a lot richer in this environment.

In order for this to become popular, it's going to have to really put the user back in control. It's going to have to deal with their concerns about too many notifications, too much junk mail. It's going to have to deal with their concerns about being interrupted by things that are not relevant to them. And perhaps more importantly it's going to have to help them feel that their privacy is preserved. And this idea that you've got all your information essentially out in the cloud and as soon as you authenticate yourself onto these difference devices, that clearly raises the issue of whether the architecture at the very core is designed so that you're the only one who controls that information. And that's been a key point of discussion amongst the people exactly how we define these schemas, how do we define the protocols and user interfaces so that privacy and security are integrated in here.

Throughout all those futuristic demos you've seen over the last few decades, there was always this concept of an agent, something working on your behalf. It wasn't just going to individual Web sites. The agent knew what you were interested in and it would, based on a set of rules or implicit things that it had learned by watching you do your work, it would work on your behalf. That concept, that actually goes back to 1945, is a very powerful concept.

Well, we now have what it takes to really build an information agent. We have XML as an interchange standard. We have rich decision software called Bayesian Inference Software that we can build down into the system that can track your usage and adjusting in an automatic fashion.

.NET is a very broad thing. There is code in Windows. There's code up on the Internet. There's code running in all the different devices that connect up here that implement access to the .NET capabilities. There's quite a spectrum of capabilities there. You can actually get at these services with a device that doesn't have anything special. If you simply have a browser, you can connect up and get to the .NET services. But it's far richer if you have a device that actually has the .NET code down on it.

So what does it look like diagrammatically? Well, you have the XML standards, then you have .NET infrastructure and then people have building blocks that sit on top of that, building blocks for things like storage, notification and identity. And every Web site can choose optionally to participate in this by offering up notifications. So if information changes that they think their user might be interested in, it doesn't just directly go in the form of emails to the user, rather it goes to the information agent that's working on behalf of that user to decide what are they doing right now, what device are they using, what priorities do they assign to information from this site that's categorized in this way, and do exactly the right thing on behalf of that user.

There's a very strong analogy here between what we're doing now and what we did with Windows. And that is, you know, what we're announcing today is more analogous to the announcement of Windows than it is to our Internet Strategy Day back in 1995. Back in 1995 we were talking about taking the world of Windows and the world of browsing and making sure that those two things worked together, making sure the Internet was going to be accessible to a lot of people. And that was a very straightforward set of steps over an 18-month period that we did to make that come true.

What we're talking about today is far more ambitious than that. This is a new platform. This will affect every piece of application code that gets written. This will redefine the user interface, what you see on the screen and how you interact, as much as the transition from DOS to Windows did. And so there's no Microsoft product that isn't touched by this activity.

If you look at the capabilities that are in .NET, for almost all of them there's an analogy in terms of what was in the operating system that we provided with Windows. For example, take storage. We've always had a file system. That's something that applications have used pervasively. If one application saves something out, it's available to the other applications.

Now that storage system was working only on the PC. And the storage system wasn't very rich. If you wanted to index those things or search them in a rich fashion, you needed to go off and use something more powerful like a specialized or general-purpose database to do that. But the idea that you had storage and all the applications could count on that storage that was part of the Windows platform.

The .NET platform has storage in a very analogous fashion. However, that storage is out in the cloud; it's not on any particular device. But the .NET platform is incredibly intelligent about replicating that storage as appropriate onto the different devices. It understands when you're connected up over a high-speed link. It understands the relevance of certain types of data, depending on which device you're using and what context you're operating in. It's also a store that's richer in the sense that the way it indexes things, the way you can search those things is more powerful. And it's actually based on database technologies. So this is what we call the XML Store, which is one element of this overall platform.

Also think in Windows about the clipboard, the fact that you could exchange information between various applications. That was a key advance that was not available in the DOS environment. Well, on the Internet today that idea of assembling information from different sources and being able to share it in that productivity world, that's a very manual operation. So here we have the idea of using XML, of gathering up the data, and integrating it together in a seamless way.

One of the big advances in the Windows environment over the years was the idea of that compound document, you know, object linking and embedding and all the infrastructure that came along with that. That's when Windows started to really become object oriented, as we got different types of embedding and we supported all the rich operations that third-party applications would bring in with those embeddings.

Well, here we have the idea of the XML data in a universal canvas. This universal canvas is the idea that you no longer leave the browser. The browser, you're always in the browser, even when you're doing your creativity work. And so we've talked about that as the universal canvas, and you'll actually see our universal canvas technology being demonstrated for the first time as part of the presentation today.

So for every element of Windows—user interface, the APIs, the hardware drivers that allowed it to work with all the different capabilities people plugged into the PC—for each one of those things there's an analogy here. But it's an analogy across all the different devices, and that includes the things that go on in the clouds.

The key principle that this becomes successful by getting lots and lots, I mean literally tens of thousands of applications that are written to it, that principle is absolutely identical. And so it's by creating those opportunities and letting applications move up to a new level that this dot-net platform will be successful.

What are these building blocks? I've already talked about the XML store, which is a very central one. Identity will evolve out of the service we have today called Passport. Notification is this idea of all the different websites tracking things that you might be interested in and delivering them to your agents. Calendar, not just individual calendar, but shared across many different people; the ability to look things up, the ability to have your software always kept up to date, those are examples of services that are completely programmable. And so just like we did with Windows we'll have development kits in our tools that let people write applications, taking advantage of these services.

We ourselves will, of course, build applications on top of these things, but as a percentage of what gets built, that will be a fairly small portion.

I want to talk about the new user experience. When we broke down the technology breakthroughs that were critical to .NET, we formed eight different groups inside the company. And each of them went off and spent several months working with the leading people in that area to decide exactly what our architecture would look like.

The team that I chose to lead was the one defining the user experience, and we had people from Windows and Office and Research and people with all sorts of different views on exactly where the user interface should go.

One of the fantastic things when you step back and think about user interface is that when you have essentially a clean sheet of paper, you can do a very rich job of taking all the things that over the last really ten years, where the user interface has simply been evolving and new things have been added to it, you can anything that's duplicative or that's proven to be, you know, that there should be just one simple way to do things and clean all of that up.

So having the new user interface is really a fantastic thing, but you've got to start at a much higher level to justify doing that; in this case, just by starting with the browser, starting by making it communication-centric, defining it in such a way that all these natural interface technologies can work with the applications that are written to this new user interface.

This user interface in a sense has to be more abstract, because the different screen sizes that we're working across here is incredibly broad. And the world of the PC in any particular year we could tell you the screen resolution we were targeting: 640x200, then 640x480, then 1024x768. You know, there was a clear target in mind there.

Well, now when you're going to have pagers and screen phones and TVs and something in the car, as well as the full-screen PC device, where even there the variety will get greater than it is today because you'll not only have the tablet form factor but there will be people who have an LCD that's literally the size of their desktop so that they get as much information viewing as possible. So we need to abstract out the idea of how do you use that display surface.

We also need to make customization something that's much more built in to the environment. We also need to take the idea that the world of files and e-mail and data, all those were really quite disparate and the commands you use to navigate those things and work with those things were really very separate. And if you look at the current user interface and say, "How many search commands do you have in your PC", the answer would be literally dozens and dozens. And sometimes it's not even clear which one to use and the dialog that comes up is very different there. So there's a lot that can be done in the user experience.

The idea of accessing the information anywhere through that store has to be defined; the idea that you can work offline and the information will be replicated down based on knowing what kind of things you want to do while you're offline, without your having to get explicitly involved to think, "Okay, I'll download this code, this file, this e-mail," all the different kinds of information that today you explicitly have to do manual work on.

Part of this is to create the creativity Web, the Web that is not just reading. And you'll find that the idea of annotation, whether it's text annotation, voice annotation, handwriting annotation, that's a fundamental capability across documents and Web sites. Your ability to create and view those annotations, this user experience file guide will define exactly what those things look like.

And so whether you're using it from the keyboard or from one of the new natural interfaces, the appearance of these applications will be quite different than the applications we have today.

I wanted to give you a little sense of this by showing you some of the elements that go into it, and, of course, a demo is the best way to really get a feel for this. So I'd like to ask Jeff Rainier to come out and show us a few examples of the natural interface element.

Jeff Rainier: Thanks, Bill. Today I'll tell you about two of the .NET user interface elements: Smart Tags and the type-in line.

Now, everybody knows that computers are really good at many things, but that there are some simple things they just don't do very well. For example, if I type June 23rd, a computer might not know that that's a date, or if I type 2:00 P.M., it might not know that that's a time. And even if it did know those two things, it wouldn't necessarily know that times and dates are useful for things like scheduling meetings.

But the .NET platform will know things like this. In fact, it will automatically recognize and categorize important words and phrases while you type them and it will turn them into smart tags. Company names, people names, times, dates, a multitude of other things will all automatically be smart tagged while you type.

Let me show you how this is going to work using some real live running code. Imagine that I've gotten a mail message that asks me to write a report. I'd probably start by gathering the data that I needed for the report. Now, today that would mean remembering which database the information I needed was in, knowing how to use that database software and probably transferring some information into a spreadsheet to do some analysis.

But the .NET UI will make this much, much easier. It will eliminate many of those steps.

Let me show you how.

Look carefully at this mail message, and in particular at Astro Mountain Bike Company here. You see that dotted blue underline? .NET has placed that there, because it automatically realized that Astro Mountain Bike Company was a company name and turned it into a smart tag. As a result, if I move my mouse over top of it a button will appear. And if I click that button a menu is revealed. On this menu are a number of actions that are pertinent to Astro because it's a company name. So from here I can go to their home page, I can look at a financial report on investor about the company or I can analyze their sales data. Let me do that.

You've seen how smart tags work in mail messages, but they're everywhere in the .NET platform, and they work pretty much the same way. Smart tags can also be personalized. This way users are able to specify what words should be smart tags, what categories they should fall into and what actions appear on that menu that you just saw.

Here in this spreadsheet mountain bike models have been smart tagged, so I can click on something like the MB3000 and get some more information about it. In this case, I can go out to my corporate intranet and look at information about this model.

But now let me show you .NET in action, recognizing smart tags.

I'll switch to a word processor and do a little bit of typing now. You can watch for that dotted blue underline to appear. That will mean that—there it is. Hanson Brothers has been recognized as a smart tag and a company name, in particular. So just like before I can get actions from this menu.

Now, one of the actions that's worth pointing out is that I can go from here to Hanson Brothers' home page, but remember I never typed a URL or added a hyperlink. This is possible because .NET noticed that companies often have home pages and knows how to get from the name of a company out to that company's homepage.

Now that I'm on Hanson Brothers' home page, you can see that there's the dotted blue underline here under this mountain bike, under the name of the company again, and even under people's names. That shows that smart tags work on the web as well, and they work basically the same way, the same menu, the same button and the same list of options.

But now let me shift gears and tell you about another .NET innovation.

The .NET user interface is powerful and more natural than past user interfaces. This natural interface is based on emerging technologies like speech recognition, natural language processing and handwriting recognition.

And one central feature of this user interface is something called the type-in line. It's right here. Now, from this place you can do a number of simple things like issue commands, open documents, search the web, but the real power of this interface applies beyond that sort of simple commanding. That's because dot-net is able to answer the questions that you asked and it's able to answer them in natural language and if you'd like it will even speak the answers to you.

Let me show you how this works. *(Typing.)*

Computer Voice: Which index would you like?

Jeff Rainier: *(Typing.)* Okay. Checking for the latest updates on that index.

Computer Voice: As of 9:10 A.M. the Dow industrial average is down minus 64 at 10,433.74.

Jeff Rainier: Did you see how the computer asked me questions to resolve ambiguity and kind of worked with me like a person might have? That's the sort of power and intelligence that's built into the .NET platform.

Let me show you one more example. *(Typing.)*

Computer Voice: How long do you want to meet? *(Typing.)* Where do you want to meet? *(Typing.)* Do you need to check my schedule? *(Typing.)*

Jeff Rainier: Ooh, I think my typo there caused some problems. Let me try that one more time.

Computer Voice: What would you like to do now? *(Typing.)* How long do you want to meet?

Jeff Rainier: Okay, this is looking more promising. *(Typing.)*

Computer Voice: Where do you want to meet? *(Typing.)* Let me see if you are both available at this time. Okay, I've scheduled an appointment with Mark Leimberg on Friday, June 23rd at 2:00 P.M. for 30 minutes in his office.

Jeff Rainier: Okay, you've seen how this interface works with typing, but this is much more natural and easier to use if you speak to your computer.

Imagine for a second using your cell phone to call in and get high priority mail messages, maybe make dinner reservations or even check for the latest news, all from your .NET server.

So I've shown you two elements of the .NET user interface today, all of which are available with typed input, spoken input and handwritten input.

I've shown you smart tags, which automatically recognize and categorize words and phrases and let you act on them.

And also the type-in line, which is just an example of the natural user interface, a centralized place for issuing commands, asking questions and working with your computer.

There are many more innovations in the pipeline. This is just a sample.

Thank you.

Bill Gates: Thanks, Jeff. That was great.

Obviously, natural language understanding is a very key element, and particularly the idea of allowing third-party applications to come in and declare exactly how they want to interact with the different utterances that are made through speech or through that type-in line. And so it's an API that is very, very critical.

Well, let me move forward with our .NET work. We're making some very exciting assumptions about what our partners, who do hardware breakthroughs, will be doing in parallel. We're not assuming that the PC or the Internet network capabilities will be standing still. And, in fact, we are dependent on a lot of these breakthroughs. We're assuming that broadband becomes more pervasive. Broadband, of course, today is very prevalent in business-to-business connectivity, but it's going to take time for that to roll out to consumers, particularly on a worldwide basis.

But some of the advanced capabilities here, where we use video streaming, we have digital meetings, some of those are there to both take advantage of and depend on those broadband advances.

We're also very bullish on wireless, and you need to break wireless down into several different categories. We've got wireless in the workplace. The buildings at Microsoft now are wired up so that we can carry our PCs around with us as we go to meetings or simply move around during the day and we're connect up at about 11 megabits wherever we go. And that kind of flexibility is very inexpensive, and I think it will be very typical for a workplace to have that.

In the home there are some new standards emerging that are going to make very high-speech home wireless networking quite inexpensive. And the ability to distribute not only, you know, photos onto a simple LCD on the refrigerator or anywhere in the house, but the ability to distribute your music, the ability even to take the PC that might be in one room and distribute out that user interface to any of those screens, that will be possible over this kind of wireless network.

Now, what that means is that your photos can all be in one place, your applications can all be in one place, and yet be available on a pervasive basis.

And those wireless networks will not have per minute charges. They'll simply be set up and you can use them as much as you want.

Now there will be wireless data in the wide area network. All the excitement there, you know, the valuations, the investments relate to the idea of moving beyond a pure voice market to a data market. Now, that data market will evolve both small-screen and full-screen devices. The small-screen devices are incredibly handy in terms of looking at a map, looking at your schedule, getting high priority messages, but it's the full screen device you'll use as you're creating documents and really browsing through rich information. So we need to make sure both of those are connected up to this wireless environment.

We're very bullish on the idea that over the next few years this wireless data capability will become pervasive as the third-generation wireless infrastructure is rolled out.

We think that authentication advances will be very important to this. Passwords are the weak link today in security systems, and so pervasive use of smart cards, in some cases complemented by biometric identification, is a really necessary element to make this all work.

You know, if people understood what a weak link a password is, I think they'd worry a lot about putting more and more information into this environment.

So really knowing who the user is is a very critical element to get established. Fortunately, the cost of those smart cards, the idea of having them standard in a keyboard reader, that's something that I think with our efforts and those of our partners is certain to take place.

The PC that we're thinking about is obviously much more powerful than what we have today. The microphone will be a built-in capability, and so a lot of the communications that you do will be real-time in nature. The idea of connecting up to somebody, editing a document together, that will just be common sense. People will wonder why it wasn't easy to do that before.

The camera won't be on every PC, but a high percentage will have it. And so that's an aspect of natural interface that the platform will support.

And PCs will have a new form factor like the tablet, but in general it will be a lot smaller and a lot more convenient. Even that kind of desktop LCD will be a PC form factor.

The small screen devices are also something where there will be incredible innovation. In many ways the power of that small screen device is greater than the power we have in the PC when we introduced Windows ten years ago. So the kind of capabilities, whether it's book reading, playing your music, dealing with photos, the kind of media richness and agent type smarts that can be down even on the small device, working on your behalf, I think they're really going to surprise people.

So let's take a quick look at what we're seeing in terms of these next generation devices. And to kick that off I'd like to ask Brian Shafer to come out and talk to us about what's a phone going to look like.

Brian Shafer: Good morning, Bill. Well, good morning. Well, we all love these myriad new devices that are coming into our lives, especially cell phones, but they all share one weakness. They tend to be islands of technology, especially those cell phones. Sure, they might synchronize in some rudimentary way with a PC, sharing phone numbers and the like, but they don't fully interoperate as well as they could with each other or with other platforms.

The .NET environment gives us the ability to address some of these issues.

Now what I'm holding here is a new class of device, a .NET device, if you will. Now, specifically this is a smart phone that we're working on with our partner Samsung and we'll be bringing it to market sometime next year.

These devices bridge the wireless telephony world that we all know and love with powerful computing, allowing us to actually extend the .NET environment down into a small portable device such as this one.

So let's take a look at what I'm talking about.

Now here you can see I have a new smart phone. Now, in this particular case, this particular phone has never been used. It has no data on it. And it's not been personalized in any particular way. And so since it's the first time use, what I'm going to actually do is log onto this device using the Passport system to give me access to the .NET environment.

Now when I log on, a lot of things are going to happen. First, all the relevant information from my personal area on the .NET server is coming down to the device, all those phone numbers, my schedules, my appointments, et cetera, even my e-mail coming down to the device. I'm also getting my personalized information being sent down as well.

So there you can see we're now up and running. So the next time I turn on this phone, this is where I'll be, everything off and running for me. I'll have my contacts and appointments there. And as you can see, it's a personalized view. So this could just as easily be instant messaging contacts or colleagues who are up and running at the moment, or perhaps some of my corporate e-mail or what have you.

Now, to be clear, I'm not just browsing at some Web site at the moment. The .NET network has actually sent down all of my information to this naked phone wirelessly based on my preferences. So no matter whether I'm online or offline I have immediate access to my information my way.

And since this is a real computer, from here I can actually control or respond to a .NET application. And you'll see some examples of that as we move forward in our presentations today.

Now, most importantly though this is a platform so our partners and our customers will be able to develop .NET or native applications for a phone such as this one.

So let's take a look at some of those native applications that are available to me. As you can see I have some powerful PIM functionality: calendar, contacts, my inbox, tasks, notes, et cetera. What I effectively have is wireless outlook available to me at any time. You'll also see that we also include Internet Explorer on these devices. So in a traditional sense I could go and wirelessly look at HTML or WAP-based data. But most importantly, however, smart phones and their cousins, the Pocket PCs, their browsers will support XML, making sure that they are full-blown participants in .NET services moving forward.

Now, I mentioned that this phone is able to interact with other devices in the .NET world, so let's go ahead and set up an example of that. I'm going to go into my calendar and pull up a new appointment. I'll set an appointment for lunch with Bill, say, next Monday. I'm going to pick the Pebble Beach Café. Now, you'll notice my preference for all the locations where I book meetings are automatically in my phone, so I don't have to sit there and type them all in three characters every number. So I'll go ahead and set the date.

And now what's happening is the phone has sensed that an appointment has changed, so it's updating the .NET server. And since I'm wireless, it doesn't matter where I am, this happens. The .NET server then takes that information and automatically federates it amongst all my other devices—and not just my devices. More specifically my colleague's Pocket PC, a wireless Pocket PC is also updated with this appointment. Or if we switch over to my assistant's PC, you can see that this appointment will now come in and be synchronized all by the server, meanwhile while I'm out running around doing my job.

So as you can see the combination of .NET services and these smart devices helps bring to life our vision of your information anywhere, anytime on any device.

Bill Gates: Thanks, Brian. Super.

Now let's turn and look at the full-screen device, in particular this tablet form factor. I'd like to ask Burt Keylie to talk to us about the work his group is doing in this area.

Burt Keylie: Hi, Bill. Thanks.

So .NET services are going to help information flow to all sorts of devices, and the smart phone, Microsoft smart phone software, in particular, is going to really enable a whole class. But there's another class of device that we think is going to be wildly popular, and this is the device that combines the visual qualities of a magazine with the handiness of a paper notebook and all the power of a PC.

So what we're going to get to talk about today and show today actually is the actual first demonstration of what Microsoft calls our vision for the Tablet PC. Okay, can you see this display?

And within the next year or two you're going to see Microsoft's partners bringing out hardware like this. This is actually prototype hardware running real software, including real Windows 2000.

So one thing about a Tablet PC is—we've looked at electronic books and you've probably heard a lot about electronic books lately. They're a type of content that really demands a better device. And I want to zoom in on this. First of all I'll show you that turning pages on this device is really as simple as turning pages in a book. So we have nothing but a book page here, and the way we turn pages is nice and very simple.

I want to zoom in. I want to show you something about the software. And this is what we call ClearType. When we talk about having the quality of paper, can you believe how paper-like those fonts were?

I'll zoom back out a little bit.

Now, the way we see it, devices, all device attempts in this class have failed to recognize the need to match paper, and so we're going to show some things here today that are .NET UI constructs that actually match the interactivity of paper.

So this is an electronic book, and I can read along and see a character. Here's "Baker", a character that's introduced at this point. In order to highlight that, remind myself of when the character was introduced, it's simply a matter of highlighting, tapping and it's done. I can place a bookmark just as simply. Oh, and I can look up a word in as simple a manner as tap on the word, tap on lookup, I see definitions for "stretched", "stretching", et cetera. A third tap and I'm back reading with no visual artifacts, no clutter.

So these are the kinds of qualities of paper that we really think that a tablet PC should be able to have.

Now, one of my colleagues is a fellow named Chuck Zacker, and he's also obsessed with this Tablet PC idea. And his obsession goes all the way back to the mid-70s when at Xerox PARC he worked with a fellow named Alan Kay, and they worked on a Dynabook concept. Chuck is on our team and he suggested to me I really ought to have a subscription to Slate Magazine. And it gives me an opportunity to show you some .NET services that support this paper-like experience.

So as I'm reading I can go to a bookstore. And look, this is integrated browsing, integrated in a way that doesn't show me stock quotes and e-mail messages and banner ads and all these other news feeds and things. I asked to see book sites and so I get a list of sites that can provide titles to the Microsoft Reader.

So one of those sites is the Slate subscription site. I can say, "Yes, go ahead and download Slate", and I get a message, the download is complete and it's in my library. So I'll just go over to my library and take a look and here it is. It showed up as the last one acquired.

Now, how do we make a book buying purchase so simple? Well, there are a few .NET services behind this, one of which, of course, is the integrated browsing.

But the second is Passport, which manages all of the transaction aspects, so that the purchase can be as simple as tapping and then watching the download occur.

The third thing is a new service called a digital asset service, which actually does digital rights management for me. In fact, it's individualizing a personalized copy of this book and downloading it into my library, and it actually has my name on the title page of the book. I know it's mine. I know it's authentic and I know I can read it on any of my devices.

So now reading books is not all we want to be able to do on a Tablet PC, right? Of course, we're going to want to check our e-mail. And to do that, we're going to want to use real Outlook. Well, at least some of us are. So here's a message from Butler Lampson. He says he's got an attachment. I need to be able to open attachments, don't I?

So open this message, open the attachment and it's a document. I recognize it. It's Charlton's interactive paper document. It's very nice and concise. But I would like to make some comments here. I think that if he could use .NET more in his discussion, he'd be following the corporate theme a lot better.

So now do I have to actually go get a keyboard in order to make comments on this document? I shouldn't have to. I should be able to simply make marks on the page. So one of the .NET services we're talking about here is the retrieval. So we're talking about i-paper as a brand. We probably could do better than i-paper. We're talking about .NET UI constructs here.

So I just want to be able to mark with my pen, put a little margin note, and I've done my markup. It's simple.

Now, one thing else I'd really like to be able to do, and I'd love to be able to do this with paper is just insert some space and write a little bit more. "Corporate tie-in". Did you notice that when I inserted the space, the annotations hung together? That was because they're smart enough to move as the underlying document changes. So when we can do things like, I can be sure that when Butler receives this back it will all make good sense. So that's a great way of using ink in a way that works much more like paper.

Now, something that I haven't been able to show you yet is the way that ink can be interactive. So to do that let's pretend that I'm in the audience and I've taken these handwritten notes about Forum 2000. And I've done a few sketches. And I want to be able to work with these notes. For example, I really thought that that smart phone was cool. I ought to be able to just select ink like I would text and highlight it. I can do that with handwritten ink and a tablet PC. I could apply bold, italicized, underlined, et cetera. There's all sorts of things we can do with handwritten ink. In fact, if I want to take a look at my notes in a much broader way I can switch my paper to college rule and see all of that ink shrink down and re-flow just as if it were text.

So I'll zoom back in to give you a little bit better look. And it's very easy to manipulate drawings with a pen. So we've got the tablet into the picture here. We're starting to develop a story, and I want to check and see whether the theme of .NET is coming together well. So to do that I'd like to be able to take the word ".NET" and just search for instances in my story. So let's see what we find.

Now, do you see what's going on here? It's searching my handwritten ink and recognizing where I've used those words, even though we haven't converted my view to text. That's because handwriting recognition is going on in the background.

So we work with my ink and we see lots of instances of .NET. It looks like it's coming together pretty well.

So one last thing, of course, I've got to have a headline for my story. And so I've got a few attempted headlines here. I'm not very good at this. If I want to see these headlines as text, it should be just as simple as saying, "Recognize that" and see them as text. Now, that's because the handwriting recognition can go in the background, but it doesn't need to get in the way of using the system, of using the handwritten ink. Only when you want to see the recognized text do you need to do that.

Okay, so that's a quick view of the kinds of things we see a tablet PC doing and I hope you all are as excited about having one of these as I am.

Bill Gates: Great. Stay tuned. Thanks, Brian.

Well, I'm certainly excited about getting one of those devices. There's really an amazing amount we'll be able to do with note-taking and sharing information and the whole structure of a meeting and the way that you have handouts in meetings and you never know, you know, whether to keep those around or if you want to change something and share that with other people in meetings.

So both note-taking and the process of meetings will be brought into a digital world and we'll have breakthrough software that's part of Microsoft Office that deals with those scenarios, which are completely new to the world of the PC.

A key point there is that was a full powered PC. That was not just a companion-limited device. That was a Windows 2000 device that ran all the existing applications and the new ones that take advantage of that platform.

Well, I've talked about .NET being in three different places. We've seen some examples of .NET software running on the client, running on the phone type device and the new form factor PC.

We've also talked a lot about these services and you're going to see quite a few of those today.

But there's a third tier here, which is the server. Today's server essentially exists in isolation. When you want to go set a server up, when you want to monitor a server, it is essentially off by itself.

But the new vision here in .NET is that those services fit into the three-tier environment, and so you can choose to run on these servers, which you may have inside your corporation or you may have out in an ASP. You can run the rich capabilities that we're talking about here.

So you can host the e-mail there if you choose to. You'd certainly typically in a corporation host your own documents, your rich, you know, creativity things in the company itself. Both for security reasons and just communications bandwidth and control type reasons that makes sense. And yet you'd want that server working in conjunction with the cloud-based services in order to make some of those documents available, assuming the right security things had been set up.

So we need symmetry between the three different levels. We need to define the semantics of security and events and mail activities and workflow around one architecture.

Another key point that we won't dive into in much detail today is that these individual servers need to have incredible scale capabilities, and all the abilities, not just scalability, reliability and manageability as well. That's something that Microsoft has been pouring a lot of R&D focus into, and we've made incredible progress, as we announced with the world-setting benchmarks around Windows 2000.

The key concept is to use software to allow the individual server building blocks to be combined together. And that's really a breakthrough for both reliability and scale.

And so that means that even in this .NET world, as the level of transactions is ten times greater than it's ever been before, the servers behind the scenes will be responding to that and able to handle that kind of load.

You want to be able to mix and match these servers we're talking about, the file servers, mail servers, database servers and with the things that you decide to just do through an ASP or through the standard .NET capabilities. And there are special things we have to do to make sure that these servers are defined for ASPs, the idea of hosting many corporate customers on a single server, the idea of taking a single corporate customer and automatically spreading their load across many servers.

Now there's a level of management capabilities there that really pushes the state-of-the-art, goes beyond what people have needed in mainframes and other systems in the past, and we need to make sure that we're pushing those horizons in the Windows environment ourselves to respond to the .NET server opportunity.

Here's a quick roadmap. Steve Ballmer is going to go through this at more length a little bit in his presentation at the end the day. So let me just summarize real quickly. There are some key elements of .NET that are actually here today, things like Passport, the XML work we're doing. The products we ship this year, what we call the 2000-generation of products, SQL 2000, Exchange 2000, BizTalk 2000, every one of those was designed around this belief that XML is very core. And it had a profound effect on every one of those designs. So there are things like that that are very here and now.

Next year a key release for us will be Windows .NET version 1. It's not the 100 percent implementation. For example, the full net user experience comes in a major release that will be at least two years off, because of the ambition that's in there.

Visual Studio 7 that we'll be previewing this year has many key elements of the .NET platform.

So next year you'll see many of the services emerge, but it will be more than two years before all the different services are out there.

And in Microsoft itself in terms of branded experiences, we have a number that will come out next year. And then the full set of services, including things like Office and Visual Studio are in the future timeframe.

So this plan is not about something that all is finished here and now, this is about how we're focusing the R&D efforts of the company and doing something that literally is as profound as the initial graphics interface work that we did quite some time ago.

So let me recap the different levels. There's been .NET services. And here the real software breakthrough work is in things like the information agent, the ability to get the information wherever you go. There's a schema that lets you keep track of what you think about music and books, and organizes things in a much richer way than has ever been done before.

Supporting offline we think is critical. Even though the Internet and all these wireless things are going to be out there, there are many cases that you're going to want to be offline, you're going to want to be able to work at length that either paying those per minute charges or without having to assume that the network is there.

The user experience, there's a lot of new elements that come into this. In some ways this is—from the consumer's point of view this is the most profound thing about .NET, the fact that we really for the first time have a platform that is designed around a natural interface, that we move away from the dichotomy of the productivity software and the browser being in two different worlds and instead move into a world that really is the best of both, and partly because we've been able to do this as a new piece of work takes everything we've learned about user interface in the last 10 years and pulls that together. You know things like when you see a table of information, there are today dozens and dozens of ways that you manipulate that table and you filter that table and in some ways there's more variety there than even in the search command I brought up as an earlier example. So coalescing that so that whenever you see a table, whether it's print or font, any type of information that's done a standard way, that's part of the style guide that goes with this new user experience.

The richness of the device is working on behalf of the user. It's not just the performance we need for natural interface, which, of course, is significant, but also things like looking at those smart tags, recognizing in the background exactly what actions you might want to take against any kind of information that's up there on the screen.

The world of programming, there's a lot of neat new things here, including the idea of the code being updated automatically. You know, the things that make the rich client complicated, those go away here, because the code and the state that you've had to manage on the PC yourself, now the .NET services are taking over that capability. The idea that you can write a simple application and just have that be hosted and available to everyone, that's really one of the founding principles of the programming platform that's created here.

The .NET devices, the new ones will be very, very important. I'd go as far as saying that the market for these small screen and other devices really can't explode until you have things like the .NET services. And in the same way that the PC really required one platform that allowed software developers to assume that that platform would be consistent and on millions and millions of devices, users expect the same thing in terms of applications in this new era and the fact that they won't be stuck with manually dealing with all this information.

So we think that by working with these device makers and making sure the software platform connect up to those things, we can take and accelerate the market for this variety of devices.

There are many of these categories, like the TV space where we've been a real leader in pushing forward what can be done there and how to redefine that experience. And we went to be involved in making sure the software connects up to all these things. This is where standards like universal plug and play can make a very big difference.

So what it comes down to is that after 25 years, Microsoft is still focused on the thing that it loves and knows well, and that is building software platforms. This is an era where what's required of that software platform is far more ambitious than anything we've done in the past. And that's why I'm very glad that we've made fundamental investments in our research group. In fact, almost every one of these new capabilities I'm talking about benefits from work that took many, many years and was off in that research environment being pulled together without a particular schedule in mind, but knowing that those capabilities would be very, very important.

So it's very fitting that in our 25th year as we've always had an idea of making these tools for more powerful, that we're attacking a new horizon, a horizon that will take even what the Internet is today and make that seem like something quite limited compared to what's possible here.

So we're very excited about it. You could say it's a bet-the-company thing. We are putting our resources behind .NET because we believe in this and so our entire strategy is defined around this platform. We are working with a lot of partners. We're very excited with the reaction they've had as we've gone through this new strategy. So let me just close by having a video from one of our key partners, Compaq, and their reaction to the work we're doing here. Thank you

(Applause.)

Microsoft .NET Framework FAQ

This article contains answers to frequently asked questions about Microsoft .NET and the Microsoft .NET Framework. The article was published in December 2000 on MSDN Online and includes both conceptual questions and run-time technical questions. The conceptual questions covered revolve around the definition of .NET and the .NET Framework, the people to whom the framework applies, where to find the .NET Framework SDK, the platforms on which the framework will run, the programming languages that it will support, the relationship between the framework and COM+ Services, the relationship between the framework and DCOM, and the difference between the .NET Framework and Windows DNA. The wide range of topics covered within the run-time technical questions include terminology, assemblies, application deployment and isolation, garbage collection, remoting, interoperability, and security.

Conceptual Questions

What is .NET?

Simply put, Microsoft® .NET is Microsoft's strategy for delivering software as a service.

An excerpt from a whitepaper on the topic briefly describes the key points of .NET:

- **Microsoft .NET platform**
  Includes .NET infrastructure and tools to build and operate a new generation of services, .NET user experience to enable rich clients, .NET building block services and .NET device software to enable a new generation of smart Internet devices.

- **Microsoft .NET products and services**
  Includes Microsoft® Windows.NET (with a core integrated set of building block services), MSN.NET, personal subscription services, Microsoft® Office.NET, Microsoft® Visual Studio.NET, and Microsoft® bCentral™ for .NET.

- **Third-party .NET services**
  A vast range of partners and developers will have the opportunity to produce corporate and vertical services built on the .NET platform.

This FAQ targets the .NET Framework, which is a piece of the .NET platform's infrastructure. See the next question to learn more about the .NET Framework.

What is the .NET Framework?

The .NET Framework is an environment for building, deploying, and running Web Services and other applications. It consists of three main parts: the Common Language Runtime, the Framework classes, and ASP.NET.

Does the .NET Framework only apply to people building Web sites?

The .NET Framework enables you to create great Web applications. However, it can also help you build the same applications you build today. If you write any Windows software (using ATL/COM, MFC, Microsoft® Visual Basic®, or even standard Microsoft® Win32®), .NET offers many advantages to the way you currently build applications. Of course, if you do develop Web sites, then the .NET Framework has a lot to interest you—starting with ASP.NET.

Where can I get the .NET Framework SDK?

The Beta 1 of the .NET Framework SDK is now available for public download at MSDN Online Downloads (/downloads/default.asp?URL=/code/sample.asp?url=/msdn-files/027/000/976/msdncompositedoc.xml). Because of its size, we offer this beta as a single download (106 MB), an 11-part download, or you can order the CD from Microsoft Developer Store:

- United States/Canada (http://developerstore.com/devstore/product.asp?productID=7597&store=Toolbox_NA)
- International (http://developerstore.com/devstore/product.asp?productID=7598&store=Toolbox_INTL)

On what platforms will the .NET Framework run?

The Beta 1 version will run on Microsoft® Windows® 2000, Windows 95/98/ME, and Windows NT® 4.0.

There is also a version of the .NET Framework called the .NET Compact Framework. It is designed to bring some of the capabilities of the .NET Framework to devices such as cell phones and enhanced televisions. The .NET Compact Framework will run on Windows CE and other embedded operating systems.

What programming languages will the .NET Framework support?

The .NET Framework is language neutral; virtually any language can target the .NET Framework. Currently, you can build .NET programs in a number of languages, including C++, Microsoft® Visual Basic.NET, JScript®, and Microsoft's newest language—C#. A large number of third-party languages will also be available for building .NET Framework applications. These languages include COBOL, Eiffel, Perl, Python, Smalltalk, and others.

What is the relationship between the .NET Framework and COM+ Services?

The .NET Framework gives you full access to COM+ services, while also making it easier to build serviced components.

.NET Framework components can be added to a COM+ application. There they can take advantage of automatic component services such as transactions, object pooling, queued components, events, and so on.

What is the relationship between the .NET Framework and DCOM?

DCOM is the COM infrastructure for cross-process communication. The .NET Framework supports a number of pluggable channels and formatters for cross-process communication. When making transitions between managed and unmanaged code, the .NET Framework uses the COM infrastructure, specifically, DCOM. All scenarios using COM+ services use managed-to-unmanaged transitions, and thus use DCOM by default. The .NET Framework also supports SOAP, the Simple Object Access Protocol, for cross-process communication where interoperability is critical.

Is the .NET Framework just a new name for Windows DNA?

No. Windows DNA is an architecture for building tightly-coupled, distributed Web applications. As the needs of distributed applications changed to require more loosely-coupled principles, Microsoft evolved the architecture to .NET. The .NET Framework is a part of the .NET architecture.

Runtime Technical Questions

Terminology

What is the Common Language Runtime (CLR)?

The Common Language Runtime is the execution engine for .NET Framework applications.

It provides a number of services, including the following:

- Code management (loading and execution)
- Application memory isolation
- Verification of type safety
- Conversion of IL to native code
- Access to metadata (enhanced type information)
- Managing memory for managed objects
- Enforcement of code access security
- Exception handling, including cross-language exceptions
- Interoperation between managed code, COM objects, and pre-existing DLLs (unmanaged code and data)
- Automation of object layout
- Support for developer services (profiling, debugging, and so on)

What is the common type system (CTS)?

The common type system is a rich type system, built into the Common Language Runtime, that supports the types and operations found in most programming languages. The common type system supports the complete implementation of a wide range of programming languages.

What is the Common Language Specification (CLS)?

The Common Language Specification is a set of constructs and constraints that serves as a guide for library writers and compiler writers. It allows libraries to be fully usable from any language supporting the CLS, and for those languages to integrate with each other. The Common Language Specification is a subset of the common type system. The Common Language Specification is also important to application developers who are writing code that will be used by other developers. When developers design publicly accessible APIs following the rules of the CLS, those APIs are easily used from all other programming languages that target the Common Language Runtime.

What is the Microsoft Intermediate Language (MSIL)?

MSIL is the CPU-independent instruction set into which .NET Framework programs are compiled. It contains instructions for loading, storing, initializing, and calling methods on objects.

Combined with metadata and the common type system, MSIL allows for true cross-language integration.

Prior to execution, MSIL is converted to machine code. It is not interpreted.

What is managed code and managed data?

Managed code is code that is written to target the services of the Common Language Runtime (see What is the Common Language Runtime?). In order to target these services, the code must provide a minimum level of information (metadata) to the runtime. All C#, Visual Basic.NET, and JScript.NET code is managed by default. Visual Studio.NET C++ code is not managed by default, but the compiler can produce managed code by specifying a command-line switch (/CLR).

Closely related to managed code is managed data—data that is allocated and de-allocated by the Common Language Runtime's garbage collector. C#, Visual Basic, and JScript.NET data is managed by default. C# data can, however, be marked as unmanaged through the use of special keywords. Visual Studio.NET C++ data is unmanaged by default (even when using the /CLR switch), but when using Managed Extensions for C++, a class can be marked as managed by using the __gc keyword. As the name suggests, this means that the memory for instances of the class is managed by the garbage collector. In addition, the class becomes a full participating member of the .NET Framework community, with the benefits and restrictions that brings. An example of a benefit is proper interoperability with classes written in other languages (for example, a managed C++ class can inherit from a Visual Basic class). An example of a restriction is that a managed class can only inherit from one base class.

Assemblies

What is an assembly?

An assembly is the primary building block of a .NET Framework application. It is a collection of functionality that is built, versioned, and deployed as a single implementation unit (as one or more files). All managed types and resources are marked either as accessible only within their implementation unit, or as accessible by code outside that unit.

Assemblies are self-describing by means of their manifest, which is an integral part of every assembly. The manifest:

- Establishes the assembly identity (in the form of a text name), version, culture, and digital signature (if the assembly is to be shared across applications).
- Defines what files (by name and file hash) make up the assembly implementation.
- Specifies the types and resources that make up the assembly, including which are exported from the assembly.
- Itemizes the compile-time dependencies on other assemblies.
- Specifies the set of permissions required for the assembly to run properly.

This information is used at run time to resolve references, enforce version binding policy, and validate the integrity of loaded assemblies. The runtime can determine and locate the assembly for any running object, since every type is loaded in the context of an assembly. Assemblies are also the unit at which code access security permissions are applied. The identity evidence for each assembly is considered separately when determining what permissions to grant the code it contains.

The self-describing nature of assemblies also helps makes zero-impact install and XCOPY deployment feasible.

What are private assemblies and shared assemblies?

A private assembly is used only by a single application, and is stored in that application's install directory (or a subdirectory therein). A shared assembly is one that can be referenced by more than one application. In order to share an assembly, the assembly must be explicitly built for this purpose by giving it a cryptographically strong name (referred to as a shared name). By contrast, a private assembly name need only be unique within the application that uses it.

By making a distinction between private and shared assemblies, we introduce the notion of sharing as an explicit decision. Simply by deploying private assemblies to an application directory, you can guarantee that that application will run only with the bits it was built and deployed with. References to private assemblies will only be resolved locally to the private application directory.

There are several reasons you may elect to build and use shared assemblies, such as the ability to express version policy. The fact that shared assemblies have a cryptographically strong name means that only the author of the assembly has the key to produce a new version of that assembly. Thus, if you make a policy statement that says you want to accept a new version of an assembly, you can have some confidence that version updates will be controlled and verified by the author. Otherwise, you don't have to accept them.

For locally installed applications, a shared assembly is typically explicitly installed into the global assembly cache (a local cache of assemblies maintained by the .NET Framework). Key to the version management features of the .NET Framework is that downloaded code does not affect the execution of locally installed applications. Downloaded code is put in a special download cache and is not globally available on the machine even if some of the downloaded components are built as shared assemblies.

The classes that ship with the .NET Framework are all built as shared assemblies.

If I want to build a shared assembly, does that require the overhead of signing and managing key pairs?

Building a shared assembly does involve working with cryptographic keys. Only the public key is strictly needed when the assembly is being built. Compilers targeting the .NET Framework provide command line options (or use custom attributes) for supplying the public key when building the assembly. It is common to keep a copy of a common public key in a source database and point build scripts to this key. Before the assembly is shipped, the assembly must be fully signed with the corresponding private key. This is done using an SDK tool called SN.exe (Strong Name).

Strong name signing does not involve certificates like Authenticode does. There are no third party organizations involved, no fees to pay, and no certificate chains. In addition, the overhead for verifying a strong name is much less than it is for Authenticode. However, strong names do not make any statements about trusting a particular publisher. Strong names allow you to ensure that the contents of a given assembly haven't been tampered with, and that the assembly loaded on your behalf at run time comes from the same publisher as the one you developed against. But it makes no statement about whether you can trust the identity of that publisher.

What is the difference between a namespace and an assembly name?

A namespace is a logical naming scheme for types in which a simple type name, such as MyType, is preceded with a dot-separated hierarchical name. Such a naming scheme is completely under the control of the developer. For example, types MyCompany.FileAccess.A and MyCompany.FileAccess.B might be logically expected to have functionality related to file access. The .NET Framework uses a hierarchical naming scheme for grouping types into logical categories of related functionality, such as the ASP.NET application framework, or remoting functionality. Design tools can make use of namespaces to make it easier for developers to browse and reference types in their code. The concept of a namespace is not related to that of an assembly. A single assembly may contain types whose hierarchical names have different namespace roots, and a logical namespace root may span multiple assemblies. In the .NET Framework, a namespace is a logical design-time naming convenience, whereas an assembly establishes the name scope for types at run time.

Application Deployment and Isolation

What options are available to deploy my .NET applications?

The .NET Framework simplifies deployment by making zero-impact install and XCOPY deployment of applications feasible. Because all requests are resolved first to the private application directory, simply copying an application's directory files to disk is all that is needed to run the application. No registration is required.

This scenario is particularly compelling for Web applications, Web Services, and self-contained desktop applications. However, there are scenarios where XCOPY is not sufficient as a distribution mechanism. An example is when the application has little private code and relies on the availability of shared assemblies, or when the application is not locally installed (but rather downloaded on demand). For these cases, the .NET Framework provides extensive code download services and integration with the Windows Installer. The code download support provided by the .NET Framework offers several advantages over current platforms, including incremental download, code access security (no more Authenticode dialogs), and application isolation (code downloaded on behalf of one application doesn't affect other applications). The Windows Installer is another powerful deployment mechanism available to .NET applications. All of the features of Windows Installer, including publishing, advertisement, and application repair will be available to .NET applications in Windows Installer 1.5.

I've written an assembly that I want to use in more than one application. Where do I deploy it?

Assemblies that are to be used by multiple applications (for example, shared assemblies) are deployed to the global assembly cache. In the prerelease and Beta builds, use the /i option to the Alink SDK tool to install an assembly into the cache:

```
al /i:myDll.dll
```

A future version of the Windows Installer will be able to install assemblies into the global assembly cache.

How can I see what assemblies are installed in the global assembly cache?

The .NET Framework ships with a Windows shell extension for viewing the assembly cache. Navigating to % windir%\assembly with the Windows Explorer activates the viewer.

What is an application domain?

An application domain (often AppDomain) is a virtual process that serves to isolate an application. All objects created within the same application scope (in other words, anywhere along the sequence of object activations beginning with the application entry point) are created within the same application domain. Multiple application domains can exist in a single operating system process, making them a lightweight means of application isolation.

An OS process provides isolation by having a distinct memory address space. While this is effective, it is also expensive, and does not scale to the numbers required for large web servers. The Common Language Runtime, on the other hand, enforces application isolation by managing the memory use of code running within the application domain. This ensures that it does not access memory outside the boundaries of the domain. It is important to note that only type-safe code can be managed in this way (the runtime cannot guarantee isolation when unsafe code is loaded in an application domain).

Garbage Collection

What is garbage collection?

Garbage collection is a mechanism that allows the computer to detect when an object can no longer be accessed. It then automatically releases the memory used by that object (as well as calling a clean-up routine, called a "finalizer," which is written by the user). Some garbage collectors, like the one used by .NET, compact memory and therefore decrease your program's working set.

How does non-deterministic garbage collection affect my code?

For most programmers, having a garbage collector (and using garbage collected objects) means that you never have to worry about deallocating memory, or reference counting objects, even if you use sophisticated data structures. It does require some changes in coding style, however, if you typically deallocate system resources (file handles, locks, and so forth) in the same block of code that releases the memory for an object. With a garbage collected object you should provide a method that releases the system resources deterministically (that is, under your program control) and let the garbage collector release the memory when it compacts the working set.

Can I avoid using the garbage collected heap?

All languages that target the runtime allow you to allocate class objects from the garbage-collected heap. This brings benefits in terms of fast allocation, and avoids the need for programmers to work out when they should explicitly "free" each object.

The CLR also provides what are called ValueTypes—these are like classes, except that ValueType objects are allocated on the runtime stack (rather than the heap), and therefore reclaimed automatically when your code exits the procedure in which they are defined. This is how "structs" in C# operate.

Managed Extensions to C++ lets you choose where class objects are allocated. If declared as managed Classes, with the __gc keyword, then they are allocated from the garbage-collected heap. If they don't include the __gc keyword, they behave like regular C++ objects, allocated from the C++ heap, and freed explicitly with the "free" method.

Remoting

How do in-process and cross-process communication work in the Common Language Runtime?

There are two aspects to in-process communication: between contexts within a single application domain, or across application domains. Between contexts in the same application domain, proxies are used as an interception mechanism. No marshaling/serialization is involved. When crossing application domains, we do marshaling/serialization using the runtime binary protocol.

Cross-process communication uses a pluggable channel and formatter protocol, each suited to a specific purpose.

- If the developer specifies an endpoint using the tool soapsuds.exe to generate a metadata proxy, HTTP channel with SOAP formatter is the default.
- If a developer is doing explicit remoting in the managed world, it is necessary to be explicit about what channel and formatter to use. This may be expressed administratively, through configuration files, or with API calls to load specific channels. Options are:
  - HTTP channel w/ SOAP formatter (HTTP works well on the Internet, or anytime traffic must travel through firewalls)
  - TCP channel w/ binary formatter (TCP is a higher performance option for local-area networks (LANs))
  - SMTP channel w/ SOAP formatter (only makes sense cross-machine)

When making transitions between managed and unmanaged code, the COM infrastructure (specifically, DCOM) is used for remoting. In interim releases of the CLR, this applies also to serviced components (components that use COM+ services). Upon final release, it should be possible to configure any remotable component.

Distributed garbage collection of objects is managed by a system called "leased based lifetime." Each object has a lease time, and when that time expires, the object is disconnected from the remoting infrastructure of the CLR. Objects have a default renew time—the lease is renewed when a successful call is made from the client to the object. The client can also explicitly renew the lease.

Interoperability

Can I use COM objects from a .NET Framework program?

Yes. Any COM component you have deployed today can be used from managed code, and in common cases the adaptation is totally automatic.

Specifically, COM components are accessed from the .NET Framework by use of a runtime callable wrapper (RCW). This wrapper turns the COM interfaces exposed by the COM component into .NET Framework-compatible interfaces. For OLE automation interfaces, the RCW can be generated automatically from a type library. For non-OLE automation interfaces, a developer may write a custom RCW and manually map the types exposed by the COM interface to .NET Framework-compatible types.

Can .NET Framework components be used from a COM program?

Yes. Managed types you build today can be made accessible from COM, and in the common case the configuration is totally automatic. There are certain new features of the managed development environment that are not accessible from COM. For example, static methods and parameterized constructors cannot be used from COM. In general, it is a good idea to decide in advance who the intended user of a given type will be. If the type is to be used from COM, you may be restricted to using those features that are COM accessible.

Depending on the language used to write the managed type, it may or may not be visible by default.

Specifically, .NET Framework components are accessed from COM by using a COM callable wrapper (CCW). This is similar to an RCW (see previous question), but works in the opposite direction. Again, if the .NET Framework development tools cannot automatically generate the wrapper, or if the automatic behavior is not what you want, a custom CCW can be developed.

Can I use the Win32 API from a .NET Framework program?

Yes. Using P/Invoke, .NET Framework programs can access native code libraries by means of static DLL entry points.

Here is an example of C# calling the Win32 **MessageBox** function:

```
using System;
using System.Runtime.InteropServices;
class MainApp
{
    [DllImport("user32.dll", EntryPoint="MessageBox")]
    public static extern int MessageBox(int hWnd, String strMessage, String
strCaption, uint uiType);
    public static void Main()
    {
        MessageBox( 0, "Hello, this is PInvoke in operation!", ".NET", 0 );
    }
}
```

Security

What do I have to do to make my code work with the security system?

Usually, not a thing—most applications will run safely and will not be exploitable by malicious attacks. By simply using the standard class libraries to access resources (like files) or perform protected operations (such as a reflection on private members of a type), security will be enforced by these libraries. The one simple thing application developers may want to do is include a permission request (a form of declarative security) to limit the permissions their code may receive (to only those it requires). This also ensures that if the code is allowed to run, it will do so with all the permissions it needs.

Only developers writing new base class libraries that expose new kinds of resources need to work directly with the security system. Instead of all code being a potential security risk, code access security constrains this to a very small bit of code that explicitly overrides the security system.

Why does my code get a security exception when I run it from a network shared drive?

Default security policy gives only a restricted set of permissions to code that comes from the local intranet zone. This zone is defined by the Internet Explorer security settings, and should be configured to match the local network within an enterprise. Since files named by UNC or by a mapped drive (such as with the NET USE command) are being sent over this local network, they too are in the local intranet zone.

The default is set for the worst case of an unsecured intranet. If your intranet is more secure you can modify security policy (with the CASPol tool) to grant more permissions to the local intranet, or to portions of it (such as specific machine share names).

How do I make it so that code runs when the security system is stopping it?

Security exceptions occur when code attempts to perform actions for which it has not been granted permission. Permissions are granted based on what is known about code; especially its location. For example, code run from the Internet is given fewer permissions than that run from the local machine because experience has proven that it is generally less reliable. So, to allow code to run that is failing due to security exceptions, you must increase the permissions granted to it. One simple way to do so is to move the code to a more trusted location (such as the local file system). But this won't work in all cases (web applications are a good example, and intranet applications on a corporate network are another). So, instead of changing the code's location, you can also change security policy to grant more permissions to that location. This is done using either the code access security policy utility (caspol.exe) or the graphical administration tool (available in Beta 2 and beyond). If you are the code's developer or publisher, you may also digitally sign it and then modify security policy to grant more permissions to code bearing that signature. When taking any of these actions, however, remember that code is given fewer permissions because it is not from an identifiably trustworthy source—before you move code to your local machine or change security policy, you should be sure that you trust the code to not perform malicious or damaging actions.

How do I administer security for my machine? For an enterprise?

Currently, the CASPol command line tool is the only way to administer security. Security policy consists of two levels: machine, and by-user. There are plans to provide a full-featured administration tool, as well as support for enterprise policy administration, as part of the first version of the .NET Framework.

How does evidence-based security work with Windows 2000 security?

Evidence-based security (which authorizes code) works together with Windows 2000 security (which is based on log on identity). For example, to access a file, managed code must have both the code access security file permission and must also be running under a log on identity that has NTFS file access rights. The managed libraries that are included with the .NET Framework also provide classes for role-based security. These allow the application to work with Windows log on identities and user groups.

The .NET Architecture: Technobabble

In this transcript, John Shewchuk, Architect for the .NET Framework, discusses what .NET means to the future of programming on the Web. The interview was published in fall 2000 on the .NET Show on MSDN Online. Topics covered in the interview include what it means to be the architect for the .NET Framework, what exactly .NET is, the extent to which Passport is an example of .NET, the productivity gains that will result from .NET, which application developers will benefit most from adopting the .NET architecture, the extent to which the user will notice a difference in using a .NET application as opposed to one that is not based on .NET, the problems involved in connecting to non-Microsoft platforms, the key concepts that people are having difficulty grasping about .NET and how it applies to their model of doing business, and the most important aspects of .NET.

Robert Hess: At the PDC in July, Microsoft had an opportunity to show developers for the first time what this new .NET architecture looked like. Now, the .NET architecture is extremely important, and there's an awful lot of facets to it. To help understand what some of that architecture is, in this episode we're going to be sharing with you architectural aspects of the .NET Framework. In later episodes we'll be talking about more different features, capabilities such as programming, services, and so forth. But this time, we'll be focusing on just the architecture. Now here to help us understand the architecture of the .NET Framework is John Shewchuk. Greetings, John.

John Shewchuk: Hello.

Robert Hess: Glad you could join us.

John Shewchuk: Glad to be here.

Robert Hess: You actually are an architect for the .NET Framework.

John Shewchuk: That's correct.

Robert Hess: And what does that mean exactly?

John Shewchuk: It means that a bunch of us at Microsoft have been working together across all the divisions at Microsoft to think about how all of the software that we're building is going to fit together to produce the overall solution, which is the .NET platform. So my job is to understand customer requirements, to think about the technologies that we could bring to bear on those customer requirements, and then work with the development teams to hook it all together.

Robert Hess: Now I suppose probably first and foremost to understand is what exactly is .NET? I mean, is it just a buzz-word? Is it just a term, just a colorful way of describing some client server interaction stuff, or what is it?

John Shewchuk: Well, .NET is an umbrella term that we're using to describe all of the new innovations that we have been working on over the course of the last three years. And largely what it is, is it's a way to take the Windows DNA architecture and all the Microsoft technologies, and we've been working to really open them up and to Internet-enable them in a very, very deep way. And so .NET describes that new world of Internet enabled Web services that give you a new way to stitch applications together to make developers more productive, and to build a new kind of application that's pretty hard to build today.

Robert Hess: It sounds on the face of it—I mean we have these Internet applications: I can go on the Internet and be on Amazon or Barnes and Noble or something like that, and they can be connecting to Visa, and you have this interconnectivity, this n-tier architecture. How is it different than that?

John Shewchuk: Well, so if you were to look at the most advanced sites out there—some of the ones you mentioned, Amazon, Barnes and Noble, and so on—the developers there are really smart folks. They've been back there building all this plumbing, and yes, they largely have many of the kinds of things they want to do with .NET. But if you think about the amount of effort that was required to put together these solutions, it's pretty enormous. So I was talking to a company down in the valley the other day that does on-line payment. They've got a developer devoted to each one of those back-end connections that they have. They have another set of developers devoted just to producing the front-end UI. And it's an enormous amount of work for them, and the solutions they produce aren't, in many ways, reusable. So once they've got that solution in place, well, it's up and running; the next time they want to do one, they have to, by hand, reconstruct that solution. So they're doing payment to Visa. Visa has a set of protocols that they need to do, and a developer has to go and learn each message that they need to send back and forth; they need to hook that up in their system in just the right ways so that all the plumbing works. What we've done is we've taken many of those things that many of those smart developers are out there doing today, and we provided a framework, a set of building blocks to make it much easier to put those things together.

So, that's kind of the first aspect, which is making it easier for developers to build these kinds of solutions. But I think there's a second, deeper aspect, which is, if you think about all the applications that you've mentioned, if I go to Amazon, I've got my Amazon password, and I've filled in my own information. Then if I go to Barnes and Noble, it's largely a different set of information that I filled in. And everywhere I go, I must have 30 or 40 different passwords, and I have...

Robert Hess: I know, I try to keep one user name and one password I use everywhere, but where's the security in that?

John Shewchuk: Yeah, exactly. Now you've got all these different islands. If you think about them, they're kind of separate apps that are all running out there, and they're not really connected together in any deep way. They may use the same Web HTTP protocol, and the same browser to get there, but there isn't a deep level of integration. But already we've started to see some examples, like Microsoft Passport. They give you a single login, and they start connecting together these sites. So I enter my user data once, and now I'm connected into a web of applications.

Robert Hess: So is Passport using .NET?

John Shewchuk: I think Passport is a great example of .NET. So when you say "using .NET," maybe that might sound a bit confusing, because .NET is kind of an overall game plan, and so when you talk about using .NET, you could be using our servers, you could be using our services, you could be using the new .NET Framework, which is a way to program, but I think of it mostly as a way to start hooking into this connection of Web services as the key thing you're trying to do when you think about moving to .NET.

Robert Hess: So then, using Passport as an example then, so Passport is not really a site you're navigating to as a user. Passport is an authority authenticator that is holding your user name and password and authentication certificates there. And someone like Barnes and Noble or Buy.com or someone like that would allow you to authenticate yourself through the services exposed by Passport. They would accept that authentication callback, or whatever. They say, "Yes, this person is who he says he is. I'm not telling you his password, I'm not telling you what all his Visa information is, just take it on our authority that he is the right person, and then move on from there." So now, Barnes and Noble is not having to write that whole "maintain this database," "maintain the user name," "maintain this other stuff," and cause you to have a new user name and password.

John Shewchuk: So again I've been talking to a bunch of companies, and it's interesting. Every company I went to would tell me about the cost associated with managing the user names and passwords. It turns out that for—on the road for the past couple of weeks, it was the number one call into their service centers was, "How do I maintain that user name and password?" So think about the expense associated with just maintaining that database. Now if you're a developer, you're probably thinking it's not that hard. All I do is I have a database, a couple of entries in the database. I hook it up to the Web page. Maybe there's a little bit of tricky stuff about getting the cookies right, and I've got to avoid the replay attacks and so on. What Passport does is it bundles all that up, and it keeps it up and running, but it also provides a bunch of infrastructure, so when you lose your user name and password, there are ways for the end user to go get that, for the developer to interact with that, and so on. So Passport is providing not just the software that you would need. They've tested it; they've integrated it with a bunch of other systems. They have processes that work; they keep it operating.

Let me give you one more example. How many sites do you go to that have community forums, where you can talk about things? Pretty common thing to do. And again, you're a smart developer: how hard is that? You go, you put a couple of entries in a database, maybe use XML files, and you hook that thing up to a user interface. But you've got to keep that thing up and running. You've got to rev it, you've got to make sure that all the sort options exist. So instead of doing that, what a lot of sites do is instead they turn to someone like MSN communities or Cy Board, and they hook those things into their site so that they don't have to do all that work. And in a way this is kind of the same thing that people were doing with component architecture, so when Windows first came out, it was a lot of work to go build a Windows app. And after a period of time you could buy things like VB controls. You could just slap them together on the page, script them together, and you could have a solution. Well, what people are doing now is they're hooking together and stitching together services to build that solution, so it's more than just the software, it's the operations, the testing, the process that goes on to keep those sites up and running, which is the really big win in terms of productivity.

Robert Hess: So the smart individuals then are thinking through what is the core fundamentals of our functionality that we expose, whether it's maintaining user database, or doing forums sort of stuff. And they embody that within a componentized architecture so that it's all nicely contained, and then some other application, some other site or whatever, merely connects up and makes calls into it and then hosts that on their own. Is it like a frame-based hosting, or how is that set up?

John Shewchuk: That's a great question. So there's a bunch of different ways you could do this. You could absolutely have those things be UI elements, and that's the way some of the simple bulletin board mechanisms work. But I think developers are going to want another level. They're going to want to control that from a code aspect. So instead of just creating a frame and having somebody else's UI show through, suppose I send that information back as XML, and I could make those calls using HTTP and XML post, get that information back, and then manipulate that in a way that I want. Integrate it with my data. Pull those things together. And that's the kind of thing that we think people are starting to move to. So already you are starting to see many sites out there starting to provide either their content or much of their information as XML available capabilities. There's a lot of work to be done, though. We've got to figure out what the business models are going to be, how to protect your site from people who want to pound on it. There's a lot of folks in the industry spending time thinking about those sorts of problems. I think we're on the cusp of a new architecture around those things.

Robert Hess: I'm just trying to wrap my head around this, speaking, like, towards the Windows programmers in our audience. It seems there's a similarity here between the old OLE controls and the next generation, which is the COM component. In the original OLE controls, it was basically a frame in your application; you had exposed Excel or Word or something like that, that the surrounding application had no control over. And then with COM based components, you could actually take and embed the components and script against those components, ask them questions, post them information. Sometimes a component actually showed visual information on the page. Sometimes it was invisible, and you were just passing information. Is it the same sort of thing?

John Shewchuk: It's exactly the same kind of thing. The only difference here is instead of that component being something that you manage each time, somebody else is going to take care of it for you. Now, you're going to have some challenges associated with that, right? The thing's going to be over on this other machine.

Robert Hess: And this other machine is across the Internet, across the firewall.

John Shewchuk: Yep. So we should at some point in time walk through the mechanisms that you use to understand that object, how you discover it, how you make the calls. But we've got that component over there. We're going to make a call to it. Well, there's going to be some things like latency. So when we talk about building things this way, it's probably going to happen at a little bit different granularity than in the OLE/COM world, where you might do it at the micro level in response to a user call. Here you're more likely to want to have things happen asynchronously. So, for example, I might have some feeds that are coming into my site, where I'm getting stock information. And then I might collect that and integrate that with my data, and then in response to a user request, display that information. So it doesn't necessarily imply the same exact internal application architecture. It's more of the model, but you're totally right on when you think about that as being analogous.

Robert Hess: So, what sort of application developers out there are going to have the most to benefit from adopting a .NET architecture?

John Shewchuk: Well, I think when we look around at the kinds of apps people are building, clearly many of the technologies we've built around things like Direct Draw and how we build end user productivity apps, things like Word and so on. All that technology still is totally applicable. None of that stuff's going to go away. Where I think we start seeing the big benefits is when you start trying to tie people together. When you start wanting to do collaboration. So, for example, let's say that we wanted to schedule a meeting together. Well, imagine if that our calendars were exposed through programmatic interfaces, so that we could write a program that could look at both our calendars, be assured that we have the right kind of privacy capabilities to be able to do that, could integrate that information and give us the solution. That's a little bit different kind of feel to the app, which is taking our inputs and maybe letting us edit a video or draw a diagram. Here what we're doing is we're getting the ability to bring together people, applications, organizations, and integrate those things, and to collaborate. And that's largely what I think the promise of the Web is. And today it's kind of interesting; it's mostly being used as a mechanism for delivering UI. And it's not until we get to this next level that we're going to start bringing people together a little bit more.

Robert Hess: So will the user actually notice a difference in using a .NET application than using something not based upon .NET?

John Shewchuk: Well, I think over time, they absolutely will know that if they are .NET enabled, there will be many benefits. Single sign-on is probably the easiest thing for people to understand. But imagine if my calendars are .NET enabled, and so that when I went to a site, and they wanted to schedule an appointment, they have the ability to drop something onto my calendar. If other sites were .NET enabled and I could, as an end user, start integrating that information, if I went to a site and instead of me filling in all the forms manually, if it could talk to my machine, and find out about the information I had available, or to other computers out there that had my information and could start stitching that together, then I think people will see a lot of end-user benefits. But I think initially the benefits are primarily going to be to the developers. So as the developer wants to go build their application, instead of having to install, manage, maintain and run each of the pieces of their solution, they'll be able to turn to other people out on the Internet, and bring those solutions together to solve problems.

Robert Hess: So, with the .NET providing this interaction between clients and servers and multiple servers and so forth like that, and the Web being such a homogenous or heterogeneous environment, what sort of problems are there involved in connecting to non-Microsoft platforms?

John Shewchuk: Well, that's a great question. Let's kind of talk about how this thing would work. So you have this great analogy of a COM component, something like a VB control, and you would put it in your form. Well, let's kind of think of an analogy between that and the way you're going to do Web services. So when you drop the control onto your machine, you installed it, and one of the things that happened when you installed it is our software would look at it, it would reflect on it, it would look at the type lib, and understand what functions were available for it. And then it would display those functions so that we could do things like statement completion, and it would integrate those things up and package them, and you'd have your solution. Well, we're going to want to do the same thing on the Web now, but those things could be running on different kinds of machines, different kinds of architectures. So at the PDC we gave people something called the Blue Book. And the Blue Book is a set of specifications that describe SOAP. So it describes the SOAP mechanism, the SOAP contract language, SCL, and the SOAP discovery mechanism. So together those things are the Blue Book, and if you went up to someone's Web site that implemented those things, you don't really need to know how it's implemented. As long as those protocols operate, you'd be able to hook that thing up. In the same way that you didn't know whether a component was written in C++ or VB, as long as it gave you the right feedback, you were able to integrate that component into your app.

Robert Hess: So you mentioned this Blue Book. Is that something that our audience can get a hold of?

John Shewchuk: Yeah, I believe that's out on msdn.microsoft.com. Look up the Blue Book. You can also go to the W3C Web site and look up the SOAP submission. That describes the way this stuff works. And there's a lot of companies out there supporting it, and all kinds of different platforms. So on Java, using Microsoft technologies based on our V6 deliverables, and then we have a really great new offering, the .NET Framework, which is in our latest V7 versions of our products. So Visual Studio.NET supports these things.

Robert Hess: Okay, I'll take and I'll get a link from you for the Blue Books and I'll put that at the bottom of the transcript window, so you can just scroll to the bottom of the transcript and find the link to the Blue Book.

John Shewchuk: So let's just say that we want to actually go do this, and we want to go hook up our Web site. Well, what's going to happen? Well, it's a pretty simple protocol. The first thing that's going to happen is that my Web site wants to talk to your Web site, so what I'm going to do is I'm going to do an HTTP request to you. And I'm just going to get your home page. Now if I looked inside the home page, just like you see style sheet links, there's going to be a link to something that's type is SCL. And so all we're going to do is we're going to follow that link, so we're going to do another HTTP request to your site, and we're going to bring down an XML document that's a SOAP contract language document, that describes the entry points to your site—so what you can call, and the order in which you might want to call it.

Robert Hess: So this document is in XML format?

John Shewchuk: Yes, it just comes back as an XML document.

Robert Hess: So SOAP is the protocol or the style...

John Shewchuk: We're not getting down to SOAP yet. All we did was we discovered what's available, and the way we do that is we go to your home page, and we look for the link to the contract language. And we bring that contract language down, and that's analogous to that type lib. And what it does is it tells us what the entry points into your site are. Now, when I want to call those things, that's when I use SOAP. And SOAP is a way to send an XML message through HTTP, and get back XML. And I said "through HTTP" because that's the typical way things will work, but all of these things are based on open Web protocols, and so if you, if those protocols get better—for example, if we have some new high performance way to do binary encodings on XML—we should be able to easily pick that thing up. Or if you wanted to use another transport, like MSMQ to send those SOAP messages, you absolutely could do that as well. So it's pretty protocol agnostic, but the common way we think people will do that, just because there's so much Web infrastructure out there, is over standard Web protocols.

Robert Hess: Plus, it gets past firewalls and stuff like that; you don't need to worry about it.

John Shewchuk: Oh, and that's great. Okay, so what I've done in my tool is we've enabled it so that if I type in, say, www.yourcompany.com, our tool will do that automatically, just like when we installed a component. So we have a new thing called the Server Explorer. You just type in the URL, and it will show you the entry points. And what it's doing is it's just doing those two requests and bringing the contract language over. What it does is it automatically builds for us the right proxies so that when we make the call on the client, we get statement completion and all those other nice things, and they're making those calls over the Web using standard protocols. And just like we were talking about, those things could be built in different languages. Well, here those things could be built in many different ways. So I mention people are building solutions in Java, they're building... IBM has a Web sphere product that supports SOAP. As long as they expose SOAP methods, the SOAP contract language in discovery, all of our Visual Studio.NET, all of our .NET platform products will be able to reach out and discover those things and integrate them. So we can certainly consume 'em, but what I think is pretty interesting is that they can also consume our stuff. So we're going to compete with folks by building really great implementations. We're going to have a great .NET framework, a great set of tools, a great set of servers, and a great set of services that are all built around this Web service model.

Robert Hess: So just seeing where this HTML is a client/server agnostic way of rendering documents, this is just delivering this same sort of thing. I mean, like Web browsers today aren't penalized because they're not working on a NeXT system, which is what it was originally developed on, but you can have Windows or Macintosh or Apache or whatever you're connecting up to. So as long as the Web server that is providing a service exposes their requested protocol in this SOAP-style format, anybody else, any client, any server, can reach over, grab that information, and find out how to post these requests for additional data.

John Shewchuk: Exactly right. So we think that openness is going to be very important to people, because we think that there's going to be lots of innovation going on, a lot of different platforms, and you don't want to... necessarily want to always have to rev your software. You may have an application or a service up and running, and you can then adjust other pieces of your application. So you get a much more loosely coupled way to build your apps, which we think can lead to a lot more productivity. So there's another aspect of loosely coupled, though, that I think is probably important for your listeners to understand. And that's that the Web architecture is very scalable. And it's scalable because there's a lot of clever things that go on behind the scenes. And we're able to take advantage of all that stuff. So let me give you a couple quick examples. When I go into a browser and I type, www.yourcompany.com, two things happen. The first thing that happens is we go look that thing up in DNS, and that gives us back an IP address, and then we take that IP address and we go talk to the machine. At both of those levels, there can be indirection. So for example, when we go look that thing up in DNS, it could send us to a data center on the West Coast or a data center on the East Coast. So we get a kind of geo-scalability in the solution. Once I'm going to that data center, I have this IP address for the solution. Well, I could have something like Cisco Local Director or the Windows Load Balancing Service send me to a different machine, so that I can scale that solution out.

Well, guess what: those same approaches to scalability, the ability to distribute the load across a bunch of replicated front ends to do things like the data partitioning on the back end—that gets me to massive Internet scale. Well, now I can use that at every level in my architecture because we're, again, using those SOAP level capabilities over those Web infrastructures to get that to happen. So we think that that's a pretty compelling aspect of the whole .NET solution.

Robert Hess: Now I know that one of the ways that sites distribute their load across things, they use them in various ways to manage a session state. Noticing that that's a person coming at them is the person who came before, thereby having an affinity to the same server they were on before, so you don't have to fetch the data from some other database and do that cross thing. Does that same session-based affinity also work with the SOAP protocols?

John Shewchuk: Well, so let's just go into that just a little bit. When you design your solution, you really want it to be stateless, in the sense that there may be an affinity to a server, but if I happened, for some reason, because of Cisco Local Director or something else, to go to some other server, everything I need in order to get the solution to happen correctly is actually encoded in the cookies or on the URL as part of the message that goes to that front-end box. So the design is one of fully stateless activity. Now I could take advantage of the fact that I'm likely to come back and cache things locally, but my design should support hitting any one of these things.

Robert Hess: Would you be penalized if your design just flatly can't address a stateless model?

John Shewchuk: I think that you're doing yourself a disservice when you build that app, because you're not going to get the highest level of scalability. But there's nothing inherent in the .NET framework that mandates that you have the fully stateless model. The great thing about our tools and our frameworks and everything is that it makes it almost trivially easy to go build these things. So you go in, you type in your function. It's automatically built in such a way that the appropriate round trips, the session states, all those things, are handled in this stateless manner for you.

Robert Hess: What are some of the key things that you're noticing people having trouble grasping about .NET and how it applies to their model of doing business?

John Shewchuk: Well, I think probably one of the... there's a couple of things that invariably come up. One is, people kind of look at the Web architecture and they look at .NET, and as they try and understand what's different, the key thing is thinking about services as a way to get more done for your developer hour, that you can go out, reach across the Internet and get that solution for you. Once they understand that, then the immediate next question is, "Okay, what's the business model? Like how does that all work?" And then two, "Wow, if every page has to go out and make all these requests for these other servers, won't my application be really slow?"

And, so the first question, on business model, let me just talk about that for a second. In the same way that you've got suppliers for any kind of business today, what happens if a supplier goes down? You go to some sort of alternate supplier. You have to think about those kind of relationships when you're building your solution. If you've got someone supplying content to your solution, you probably want to have alternative ways to get that information in the event that they're down. So there's going to be many different approaches that people use. Some people will cache information. Some people will have alternative suppliers. Some people will just make very sure that their suppliers have very good reliability, by maybe having service level agreements with them. So, there's many different ways that people are going to approach the business model part of the equation, and I don't think we have an answer per se at Microsoft; the community as a whole is going to go out and figure these things out. And I think it's just like when people first started building package software, or people started doing the Web, nobody really knew what the solutions were going to be, but there's a ton of really smart people out there, watching the show today, they're going to be the folks who figure that stuff out. And they should come to us and ask us about the infrastructure that they need. We'll do that, other vendors will do that, but I think it's going to be a pretty organic thing about the business models.

Robert Hess: So we're not defining the business, we're simply enabling people to define their own businesses.

John Shewchuk: Exactly. And I think that they're going to have just the same kind of challenges that they've always had. If Visa's down and can't process your credit card, what do you do? People come up with ways to handle that inside their businesses.

Now, the second question, which is, "How am I going to handle a request that comes into my page if I'm going to have to handle all these requests to the back end?" And again, we're going to see a lot of different solutions. One of the approaches is to make those things happen asynchronously. So, for example, you might make requests out of band. So if you're doing a stock market page, you might have the stock market information coming in from your supplier, you might aggregate that into a local database, and then as your page requests come in, display that. But that's still using a .NET architecture, on the back end, to go do the information. You might, just like we talked about in the previous example, have a service level agreement, where you work with your supplier to have very high-performance connections, so that you can get that information done in a timely way and display that information to your customers. So as customers start thinking about how they're going to integrate these other vendors, to give their customers those solutions, then people seem to get pretty excited about it. Like, "Oh, I get it. You're providing the infrastructure and some approaches to get the solution done, not the one way to go do this kind of thing."

Robert Hess: Not to scare off some of the potential service providers there, but let's say you had a site and you had a service contract of some service providing the Visa model. And that service provider just started not having good service. Their servers are down all the time; it was a slow connection. Because of this .NET architecture, it wouldn't really cost you, as the consumer, the site that was consuming the services, that much trouble to switch to some other service provider?

John Shewchuk: I think that one of the ways that vendors will differentiate themselves is they are going to have a lot of cool stuff running in that solution. What we're going to do is we're going to raise the level. So instead of you having to worry about how do I encode the bits over the wire, what you want to do is you want to think about how you're service is much better than the other guy's service, in terms of real value to your customers. The value's not going to be as much in kind of the lowest level plumbing, how you connect those things up. And if that's the way you think you've got a lock on your customers, then I think you've got some stuff to worry about, because that's not really helping your customers. Your developers want to have easy solutions at that level, and they want to take advantage of what you really bring to the table.

Robert Hess: Thanks. Now before we wrap things up here, are there any key concepts about .NET that you think is really important for the audience to grasp?

John Shewchuk: Well, I just love to walk through kind of the main differentiations about .NET. So we talked about the open Internet protocols; I don't think we need to say too much else there. I think it's worth pointing out that Microsoft is going to be taking all of our server products, things like SQL, and Exchange, App Center, and we're going to .NET-enable those thing, and that means we're going to support these open Internet protocols, things like SOAP, so you'll be able to call, and over time they're going to become all programmable with the .NET Framework. In terms of our services, we're going to be doing the same thing. So the things that Microsoft runs, things like Passport, our calendaring services, our storage services, those things will become .NET enabled and programmable. The other key thing is we're going to have our services and our servers over time be able to work together better, to be able to federated and be able to use common models.

Robert Hess: By "federated..." what do you mean by federated?

John Shewchuk: By federated, let's take e-mail as an example. Well, you can use Hotmail out on the Web, and let's say it's fully SOAP and Web service enabled. Well, I might want to use those same models against my local exchange system. You could think of an exchange and Hotmail, when they use the same Web service model, as being different levels of capability. You'd want those things to talk to each other, so one's kind of the corporate accelerator, and one's a general mass-market solution. When they work together well, you can think of those things as being federated together. So, we've got a set of federated servers and services; we want people to think about taking their apps and making them .NET enabled, turning them into services so that other people can use them. And when you do all of these things, you get increases in productivity, you get the ability to more easily integrate with other folks' stuff. I think there are other kinds of interesting opportunities. For example, on the UI side of the house, what you'd be able to do is clearly we're going to let you project HTML out and support cell phones and all that kind of stuff, but imagine that you have much smarter clients. They'll be able to use the Web service that you provide to start putting together solutions in ways that maybe you as a developer didn't even think about. So when Excel or Word becomes programmable, people inside the corporations use that programmability to build solutions for their internal customers. I think you'll start seeing the same kind of thing.

So .NET gives us the ability to produce those much more capable custom solutions, to integrate other folks' stuff, to leverage other technologies that are running out on the Web, to be more productive, to integrate with other solutions. So I think there are a lot of pieces to .NET, and hopefully this has given your audience a kind of top-level understanding of some of those things.

Robert Hess: Well, thanks, John. I appreciate you spending the time with us to share with us your thoughts as the .NET architect, what .NET means to the future of programming on the Web, whether it's on a Microsoft Windows platform or integrating with some other platform out there on the Web, which the Internet is so great at incorporating. So, that covers the architecture of what the .NET Framework provides to you. Now, after this short break, we'll take and we'll come back and talk with Mark Anders to try to dive in further to some of the programmability capabilities for what you as programmers need to start thinking about in order to enable your application solutions to use the .NET architecture.

The .NET Architecture:
Enter the Programmer

In this transcript, Mark Anders, Product Unit Manager for the .NET Framework, discusses the issues that programmers will face in writing code for the .NET Framework. The interview was published in fall 2000 on the .NET Show on MSDN Online. Topics covered include how .NET makes programming and accessing system resources simpler, how .NET allows code from different programming languages to be mixed, how the programming experience has been made consistent across all of the different types of applications and services, how .NET has made server-side Web programming similar to programming in Visual Basic, the new programming language that has been created (C#), what a common language runtime is, and how .NET provides a simple, clean, and consistent way of building highly scalable applications that also interoperate with non-Microsoft systems.

Robert Hess: The .NET Framework is more than just a bunch of high-level overview thoughts and concepts of servers and services and Web pages and stuff like that. Because at some point in time, you've actually got to write code. Now to help us understand the issues that a programmer's going to face in writing code for the .NET Framework, we have with us here Mark Anders. Mark's a Product Unit Manager for the .NET Framework. Thanks for joining us, Mark.

Mark Anders: Thank you.

Robert Hess: So, in a programmer's perspective, what does the .NET Framework actually bring to the table?

Mark Anders: Well, what the .NET Framework really brings to the table is that it makes it, number one, easier for you to write your code. It frees you up from the plumbing that you have to write in the past. And it also gives you a consistent way of writing applications that take advantage of windows that integrate with Web services, that expose Web services or that are Web-based applications. So you have sort of a consistent, very, very much easier to understand, far-less-code-than-you-had-to-write-in-the-past way of building applications.

Robert Hess: And by "easier," what exactly do you mean? What was harder in the past and how are you making it easier with the .NET?

Mark Anders: In the past there were really a couple of things that, depending on the type of application that you were writing, that made it difficult. If you look at how we defined APIs in the past, there were really a bunch of different ways that you could access the system. For example, we would have the Win32 APIs, which were a set of low-level function calls with some data types like an HWND, or a handle to a brush or something like that. And that was one level of the system. Then, depending on the language, there were different frameworks that were built up to provide an abstraction that programmers typically programmed to. So for example if you were a VB developer, you thought in terms of rapid application development with controls and event handling. If you were C++ developer, you thought in terms of something like MFC, with inheritance and a very C++ orientated way of building Windows applications.

Robert Hess: So then the whole thing was .NET, and it takes all these different models and different approaches to writing applications, and simplifies everything?

Mark Anders: Well, what it does is, number one, it simplifies it. So if you think about COM programming and the type of way that you programmed COM in terms of implementing a variety of interfaces, in terms of managing the lifetime of objects, we've simplified that so you that you don't have to think of the plumbing anymore. We've also enabled it so that across all of the different languages there's a single consistent way that you access these system services.

Robert Hess: So you mean like if I was a VB programmer, doing new .NET VB programming, and I looked at some C code or some ASP code, I could actually recognize what they were doing a lot easier? It would almost be the same sort of language format, or what?

Mark Anders: Yes, exactly. So that the layers of the system are, we've got the .NET Framework, which is sort of the programming constructs that you use. So whether you're in VB or C++ or C#, which is the new language that we've introduced, the programming framework that you use is the same. So when you create a window in one, it's a window in all of the others, and you can mix the code between all of those different languages.

Robert Hess: Yes, because I can remember when I first got started, I was doing Win32 programming, and when Visual Basic came out I looked at how they did it. Everything was different. I didn't have a message loop in Visual Basic; I didn't have a "CreateWindow" call; I didn't have to do that anymore. So all of the things that I learned to do for Windows programming in Win 32 was basically thrown out the window when I had to do VB programming, and then with ASP programming, it was a whole new ball of wax. So you're saying the .NET Framework creates an abstraction layer of what the system provides. It's the same for all those people?

Mark Anders: That's true. There were these different layers that you programmed at. But the fundamental thing about .NET is to really pop up a level. So what we have done is we've simplified it, made it consistent across all the different types of applications that you've written. The big focus for .NET is really this next generation of Web applications and services that we enable. And we also enable you to build Windows applications, but we've made it so the programming experience is really consistent across all those different types of applications and services. So why don't I actually show you some code of how we would build some Web application, using the .NET Framework and ASP+, which is a part of the .NET Framework?

Robert Hess: Sounds like a good idea.

```
<form method="post">
<h3>Name: <input id="Name" type=text>
Category:
<select id="Category" size=1>
    <option>Communications</option>
    <option>Deception</option>
    <option>Travel</option>
</select>
<input type=submit value="Lookup">
<br><br>
</form>
```

Mark Anders: So this is just some very simple HTML that we have here, right? And the thing about the Web programming model has always been that it's a stateless programming model. You have HTML that gets sent down to a browser. You've got something like ASP, which is all about script code. And so if we take this HTML page, it has a simple form with an input box. Let's take a look at that in the browser. This is that page. And you'll notice if I do something like key in my name or select deception... and what I'm doing here is I'll build up an application that's selling spy equipment. That's why the categories are a little unusual. If I click Lookup, what I get back is just the same thing I started out with, because it's just HTML. I'm posting back to that page. If we look at how we would do something with that page, for example, grab the values that I entered, and display a message to the user, and then also you'd probably like it so you didn't lose the values from the edit box and the drop down. If you look at how we would do that using our existing methodologies, it would look something like this.

Robert Hess: The ASP code on the server: that is then extracting the data, pushing it back forward again.

Mark Anders: The key point of what was happening was in order for anything to happen, you have to write code to make it happen. HTML has no built-in functionality to display a message or maintain the values. It's all just a document, and you play games with having server-side logic that generates the right stuff to give you, the user, experience that you want. And it means that you have to write a lot of code. So, here, let me show you that page. I'll show you what it does. If I type in my name, and I say that I like travel, you'll notice that it says, "Hello, Mark, you've selected travel," and it maintains the values. The way that I did that in ASP code is I had to write code for every little thing that I wanted to happen. So when I'm outputting the input, I have to grab the name from the request that came in the HTTP request, and shove that in the input field to say this is its value. Doing the select, I had to do quite a bit more code. I had to say, "Is the particular option that the user sent me the option I'm spitting out?" If so, I label that as selected. And to actually spit out the message, I just plop a little "if" statement in there that says, "Hello," whatever the name was. And that's the style of ASP code that you wrote. And it's actually very easy for people, right? You just save that file on the file system, and the system automatically compiles it when you request it with a Web page. And so it's pretty straightforward, but there's a lot of code that you have to write.

```
<form method="post">
<h3> Name: <input name="Name" type=text
<%= "value="+Request("NAME") %> >
Category:
<select name="Category" size=1>
    <option <% if Request("Category") = "Communications" then
    Response.Write("selected")
    endif %>>Communication</option>
    <option <% if Request("Category") = "Deception" then
    Response.Write("selected")
    endif %>>Deception</option>
    <option <% if Request("Category") = "Travel" then
    Response.Write("selected")
    endif %>>Travel</option>
</select>
<input type=submit value="Lookup">
<br><br>
<% if (Request("Name") <> "") then %>
Hello <%= Request("Name") %>, you selected:
<% Response.Write(Request("Category"))
end if
%>
</form>
```

And also, if you go back to that VB example that you were talking about in terms of VB forms and not thinking about message loops: you just thought of a form, and you thought of event handling. You thought about the controls that you were going to use, and what you wanted it to accomplish. And so if you were a VB developer who went to Web development, you would say, "Well, what is all this stuff?" Well, the language might be the same, or you could use VB script in there, and that's pretty similar. But the programming techniques that you used were very, very different. And if you were a C++ developer, I wouldn't be able to write ASP at all, because it was script language. So I would have to write at the ISAPI level, and do a lot of low-level code. And what we really tried to do with the .NET Framework is, first of all, raise the level of abstraction, so that if you're a C++ developer or a Visual Basic developer, you have a really consistent way of viewing the entire system, and also, to take the programming model and make it so that whether you're programming a Windows client or you're programming the Web, it feels the same. You have the same programming construct.

Robert Hess: So you're programming a Windows application the same way you'd program a Web page?

Mark Anders: Well, actually its kind of the reverse. It's more that we take the techniques that we've used to really simplify Windows development and apply them to Web development. So if you think about writing at the Win 32 level, it's pretty low-level code. You've got a Win proc and you've got a message loop, and you think about all of that. The frameworks that were built that people typically target, such as VB, such as MFC, are higher level constructs, where a lot of the details of how that happens, how you interact with the message loop, how events come in...

Robert Hess: Are being handled for you by the underlying OS.

Mark Anders: Right. There's the message map in MFC, and there's some mechanism in the VB form that dispatches, that hides it from you. Now, with a good framework, though, you can actually drill down, and if you need to get at that lower level, you can. So let's take a look at how you would build that same page in ASP+. So if you think about Windows and what you've done with VB, you had this notion of controls that had properties, methods, and events, and you would interact with those controls. So what we've done with ASP+ is that we have taken those same concepts, and applied it to Web development. So we have the concept of the server control, and what that is is, it's an object that runs on the server, it's a control that runs on the server and that I can program against. And it performs the same function in a Web app that it does in a Windows application, which is that it displays the UI to the user; it generates the UI. And it also interacts with the user, so as they interact, as they click on a button, that control, for example, that is the button control, can handle that, and then raise events.

Now the way that we represent this probably still sounds a little mysterious. A server control: what is that? Really what it is is it's a tag. It's represented by a tag with an attribute "runat=server". So what a server control is, is a control that runs on the server, and it's represented by a tag with an attribute of run at equals server. So I can simply go up to that input and simply add this "runat=server" attribute.

```
<input id="Name" type=text runat=server>
```

Robert Hess: That's the same like in scripting code. In my scripting I can say "<script runat=server>" and that's server-side script.

Mark Anders: Exactly. That was one of the techniques that was used in ASP to denote server-side code, and so we took the same technique and applied it to tags. When the ASP+ compiler sees that, what it does is it says, "Instead of having this tag and spitting that out to the client, I will instantiate this control that's responsible for generating this UI that goes down to the client to represent that input tag," for example. And it will also do some other stuff for us.

So let me now switch to a page where I've added run-at-server to all of the different tags that we want active on this page. And as you can see, I haven't written any code; I've just added this one attribute in a similar manner to how I would possibly build a VB form. I would drag a bunch of controls, I haven't written any event handlers. But now if I run it—so I'll save that, and switch to this. And so now if I run that, and say "deception," you'll notice when I request it, the values are maintained in the various controls. Because the controls can interact with the action of posting back, and they can understand, for example, the values that I, as a user, have input.

```
<form method="post" runat=server>
<h3>Name: <input id="Name" type=text runat=server>
Category:
<select id="Category" size=1 runat=server>
    <option>Communications</option>
    <option>Deception</option>
    <option>Travel</option>
</select>
<input type=submit value="Lookup" runat=server>
<br><br>
</form>
```

Robert Hess: So then what was happening there is that you were having input code, input tags being stuck on your client-side page that came down to your client. You hit the submit button; then when that posted back to its own self, you had server-side code that is being run just because you said "runat=server" that each input item grabbed its value out of incoming item, and reiterated itself back out to the client page again.

Mark Anders: Yes, exactly. So the way the model works is exactly that. We compile the page down to—it's actually an object that is the page and all of its controls that run on it. And we instantiate it to handle the incoming requests. It looks to see if any values have come back from the client. Each control can take part in the request processing. So the input control can look and say, for example, "Did my value come back?" And if so, I can grab that and make that available. And when I regenerate the page, it can spit out the proper value.

Now the other thing that you can do is that you can actually, from a programming standpoint, write code that interacts with those controls. So if we go and take a look at how we would program against this, in VB what I would do is I would write a little event handling code to say when the button is clicked on, I would like my code to get called, and we can do the same thing.

So where we would—the first thing we would do is we would probably place a label control on the form. And I can do sort of the equivalent thing in ASP+, and I'll add a little label, which in this case is an HTML span, also with that run at server attribute. And you'll notice that I have an I.D., which is the programmatic identifier that I use to address the control from code. So I can then drag a little event handler. And here I'm using Visual Basic code. One of the key differences about ASP+. ASP is that we can support all of the different languages that target the .NET Framework. So we can use Visual Basic, full Visual Basic, not VB script. We can use C# as a language. So in the past, ASP has also been about if you wanted ASP developer experience, you used script languages, and they were loosely bound, and you didn't have all of the features that you had in VB. Here you have actually the full VB language, and it's actually compiled. It compiles down to native code, so it's much more faster.

```
<script language="VB" runat=server ID=Script1>
Sub SubmitBtn_Click(Sender as Object,  E as EventArgs)
Message.InnerHtml = "Hi " & Name.Value & _
                    ", you selected: " & _
                    Category.Value
End Sub
</script>
<form method="post" runat=server>
<h3>Name: <input id="Name" type=text runat=server>
Category:
<select id="Category" size=1 runat=server>
    <option>Communications</option>
    <option>Deception</option>
    <option>Travel</option>
</select>
<input type=submit value="Lookup" runat=server
    OnServerClick="SubmitBtn_Click">
<br><br>
<span id="Message" runat=server></span>
</form>
```

Here's a little event handling function. And what I'm doing with it is simply going out to the controls, so I go out to the input, which is the I.D. "Name," and I go out to the select. I retrieve their values, and then I set the inner-HTML, the span, which is my little label, to be equal to the message.

Robert Hess: And the inner-HTML, that's the same property I would use in dynamic HTML, and the client using Internet Explorer, but I'm doing it on the server rather than on the client browser.

Mark Anders: Exactly. Now, the key thing to note there is that we do not have the full DHTML object model. It's not really DHTML; it's something that's tailored at the server and had a slightly different object model. Where possible, we've kept it the same, so if it's a span control, if it's a span, you actually have inner-HTML and the same properties. We've tried to keep the properties the same so that you can leverage that knowledge. But it is slightly different.

And so the last thing I can do is I have to tell the system that I want my method to be called when I click on the button. So I add a little event binding to the button that says, "For your on-server click event"—an OnServerClick as opposed to OnClick, which is the client side click event, called the submit button click.

```
<input type=submit value="Lookup" runat=server
    OnServerClick="SubmitBtn_Click">
```

And so if I save that, and then re-request this page, it'll say, "Hi, Mark, you selected deception." And if we look at the HTML code that was generated in the client side, if we do a view source, you'll notice I don't get any of the server side code that I input. And I don't see "run at server." It's simply HTML.

Now one of the things that you'll notice is that there is a hidden field here. Even though we have a model that feels very much like VB on the server, or C++ with something like MFC, the programming model is actually stateless. So even though it feels stateful on the server, it's actually stateless in that when you actually finish generating a page, we destroy the instance of the classes that generated that page. And that means that if you're scaling your application in a Web farm, you can have multiple machines, and the request can come in to any machine. What happens is all the controls, if they need to store states between one invocation and another, can do so, and it's actually sent to the client.

Robert Hess: So it can be a stateless application to an extent, but still have a stateful feeling to it.

Mark Anders: Exactly. The programming model is stateful. And if you think really about what people do on the Web today, they play games to get around the fact that it's stateless. That there is no state that really held on the server, because with a Web application model you want things to be stateless.

So this gives you a view of how we've made server-side Web programming similar to VB. And it's actually a much richer architecture. I'd love to come back some time and show you more about the power of that. But the other thing that we've done is we've made it so that writing applications of any type, accessing system resources of any type is much, much simpler. So that in the same way that I just simplified a bunch of ASP code with ASP+ code, we can also use the .NET Framework to simplify doing things like writing to the NT event log.

Robert Hess: Standard Win 32 stuff.

Mark Anders: Standard Win 32 stuff. So I can show you a little code here. So if I wanted to write something to the NT event log, this actually came from MSDN; we went there to figure out how to do this, for a little sample. There's a lot of code that you have to write. You have to register event sources, you've got to do things with the account, you've got to then finally write something to the event log.

```cpp
// GreetingsTest.cpp
#include <windows.h>
#include <stdio.h>
#include <tchar.h>
#include "..\Greetings\Greetings.h"
int _tmain(int argc, TCHAR** argv)
{
    if (argc == 2 || argc == 3)
    {
        LPTSTR strUser;
        if (argc ==2) strUser = _T("Guest");
        else          strUser = argv[2];
        HANDLE hEventLog;
        hEventLog = RegisterEventSource(NULL,
            _T("Greetings"));
        PSID pSid = NULL;
        DWORD dwSidSize = 0;
        SID_NAME_USE eUse;
        LPTSTR DomainName = NULL;
        DWORD dwDomainName = 0;
        LookupAccountName(NULL,strUser, pSid,
            &dwSidSize, DomainName, &dwDomainName,
            &eUse);
        pSid = (PSID)new BYTE[dwSidSize];
        DomainName = new TCHAR[dwDomainName];
        LookupAccountName(NULL,strUser, pSid,
            &dwSidSize, DomainName, &dwDomainName,
            &eUse);
        ReportEvent(hEventLog,
            EVENTLOG_INFORMATION_TYPE, CAT_GREETING,
            MC_HELLO, pSid, 1, 0, (LPCTSTR*)&argv[1],
            NULL);
        DeregisterEventSource(hEventLog);
        delete [] pSid;
        delete [] DomainName;
    }
    return 0;
}
```

Robert Hess: And doing stuff to the event log is actually something that's fairly important, and we recommend applications that should be doing this to definitely make sure they do it, because it allows the system to work well, for the administrators to find out what's going on and to notice how to tune their systems properly. So this is very important code to do, and yet it's also difficult to do.

Mark Anders: Right, exactly. And this, unfortunately, is kind of typical of a lot of the stuff we've had in the platform. A lot of the things that you would like to be very easy to do require a lot of code.

Robert Hess: One of the problems being difficult, I would suspect, also means that quite often people do one of those steps slightly wrong, and it ends up causing a problem or a bug in their application.

Mark Anders: Exactly. I mean, for every couple of lines of code that you write, you could introduce a bug. And if you have to write 20 lines of code, you have 20 opportunities to introduce a bug. If we take a look at how you would write the same thing in the .NET Framework, this is it.

```
using System.Diagnostics;
public class GreetingsTest{
    static void Main(){
        string message = Environment.GetCommandLineArgs()[1];
        EventLog myLog = new EventLog();
        myLog.Log = "Application";
        myLog.Source = "GreetingTest";
        myLog.WriteEntry(message);
    }
}
```

Robert Hess: A lot less code.

Mark Anders: It's a lot less code. And the other thing is you can go up to this after it's been written. It's not only a lot less code to write, but if you're somebody who's maintaining a site, an application, you can go up to that and look at it and it's very, very straightforward.

Robert Hess: You're just creating an event log object and accessing it. Now I also notice this is using C#.

Mark Anders: This is using C#, which is a new language that we've created that takes the power and expressiveness of C++ and makes it much simpler. And it also works with the new common language runtime, which is really the lowest level of the .NET Framework, and really what all of this stuff is built on.

Robert Hess: What exactly is a common language runtime?

Mark Anders: What the common language runtime does is it takes care of all of the plumbing that you would normally write, so if you know COM, and you would think about IUnknown, you would think about implementing IUnknown for discovering what interfaces you have, and doing AddRef/Release for managing the lifetime of your objects. And if you wanted to, for example, be usable by VB client, you would use automation so you would implement IDispatch. The common language runtime is the thing that takes care of all of that for you.

Robert Hess: Is it kind of like MFC or ATL?

Mark Anders: Well, it's kind of, it's more like how a language represents a class and an object, and fundamental. MFC is really a framework built in C++ for doing a certain type of application. ATL is really a framework for, in C++, doing COM. The runtime is really the way that any language—whether it's VB, C#, Java script, COBOL—can have an object system or a type system that is common across all those languages. And it gives you lots of...it simplifies the code that you have to write, it makes it so that you have many more powerful features such as language inheritance. I can now actually use implementation inheritance so I can just say now I'd like to extend this object and override a method or add a property. The cool thing about it is that it's common across all the different languages, so that an object in one language is an object in another language. So if I'm in VB and I create an object, and it has some properties, methods, and events, and I go into C#, I can see that object as if it was a natural C# object; I wouldn't know that it's any different.

Robert Hess: And does the language itself have to uniquely support the notion of objects? What if I had a language like Forth or something like that that doesn't really understand objects? Could I use the common language runtime with that? Would I have to enhance the language to support objects? Not that people are writing in Forth anymore, but I used to.

Mark Anders: There are actually a lot of languages that are targeting the .NET Framework in the common language runtime: things like APL, which is another language that you don't hear many people writing in. But there are actually communities where people do. There are a variety of different levels that you can support the common language runtime.

Robert Hess: What's the benefit, then, of having a common language runtime that can allow APL, PL1, Forth, or things like that to still be used?

Mark Anders: Well, the real benefit is, as we've gone around to customers who use different types of languages and find out why they use them, typically it's because those languages allow them to express the concepts that they are trying to express more concisely, and be more productive than other languages. So if you go to Wall Street, for example, they might use specialized mathematical language, like a APL or Maple.

Robert Hess: Or FORTRAN or something.

Mark Anders: Or FORTRAN. And they do it because it has unique attributes that make them more productive. If you look at why Visual Basic has been popular, or why C++ has been popular, it's typically because the languages have a certain expressive power, a certain way of expressing syntax and certain facilities that make it more productive and easier for people to understand.

Robert Hess: So then with C# kind of being a language that we're describing as being well-tuned for the .NET Framework, we're not necessarily trying to say that everyone needs to rewrite all their applications for C#. C# is just a language they can use.

Mark Anders: Absolutely not. We've also modernized VB quite a bit, to give it a lot. So now in VB.NET, you have things like inheritance, you have exception handling. So we've actually taken all of the languages that we've produced, and we've made it. VB is as good as C#. C# was to take the C programmer, the C++ programmer, and give them a more productive language, with a syntax that's familiar. But it doesn't mean that everyone has to write in C#. In fact, the whole reason that we've invested in a multi-language platform is to say that people have very real reason for using multiple languages.

Robert Hess: When I was talking with John earlier, and he was talking about the whole notion of services on the Web and client/server interaction and SOAP and exposing your methods and protocols in that fashion, it seemed very much like .NET was being this big network connectivity platform. So far what we're talking about is individual granular bits and pieces, whether it's the common language runtime or whether it's this runat=server stuff with ASP+, or whether it's C#. And individually when I looked at all those different pieces, I'm not necessarily seeing this Internet connectivity model.

Mark Anders: Right, we haven't seen anything about Web services. Well, the .NET Framework actually provides a very, very simple way to create and consume Web services. And I can actually quickly show you how you build one of those, as well. And I realize we're getting towards the end here, so I'll have to make this quick. So this will be the fastest Web service you've ever seen. What we've done here is we've created in the same way that ASP created a model for building HTML pages, where you write some HTML and you add code. We have a similar model for Web services, but the model is really that you write classes and deal with data, and we map in incoming HTTP requests with SOAP or HTTP-Gets or Form Post into method invocations, and we hide the fact; we make it so that you don't have to think about XML or how the data came in. You get to think about the data that you want to deal with, and the data that you want to return. So for example, the first thing I would do is... we have a new type of page, which is an ASMX page.

```
<%@ WebService Language="C#" Class="Demo" %>
using System;
using System.Web.Services;
public class Demo {
}
```

And the first thing I'm going to do is to define a class. What we're using here is C#, and we have a little declaration that tells the ASP+ runtime that we're programming in C#. And now if I go and request that page, by hitting that URL, we dynamically compile it, and because we realize it detected that we're hitting it with a Web browser that is not invoking a Web service, it actually generated a little HTML help page that gives us information that this was a URL that was really a Web service. And it gives us the name of the Web service.

Robert Hess: It's almost like self-documenting?

Mark Anders: Exactly. It gives you a little documentation page, and allows us to see what the contract is, the SCL contract. And if I request that, it will return the XML that describes what my Web service does. Since we haven't actually added any methods to the class, it doesn't actually do anything at this point. It doesn't say much, but it has the outer wrappings. So now if I go and add a method, for example a method to take two numbers and add them together or return them, I can simply add that.

```
<%@ WebService Language="C#" Class="Demo" %>
using System;
using System.Web.Services;
public class Demo {
    [WebMethod]
    public int Add(int num1, int num2) {
        return num1+num2;
    }
}
```

Now a couple things to note, one, there's no XML here. My business logic in this case, although it's not very proprietary or valuable, is adding numbers. So I think of just taking two—

Robert Hess: You're going to make an awful lot of money on the Web like that.

Mark Anders: Yes, exactly. I guess I wouldn't quit my day job anytime soon. So I'm just taking two numbers, and I'm thinking of adding them together and returning them. And so that's how I've written my method. I don't have to think about HTTP or XML. I think in the data types that I naturally think in, and the Web service programming abstraction takes care of all the details. So if I simply save that, and refresh this page, you'll notice that the HTML document invocation page got a lot richer, and it tells me that I now have an add method, and it tells me the parameters. And if I go and view the contract now, you'll notice that that, too, has gotten much richer. So we take care of all of the mapping of how you take data types and map them into XML and how you take services and expose them, and the plumbing. Again, this the theme of getting rid of the plumbing, so you don't have to think about, "How do I take this class and generate this type library for the Internet; I just think of writing the class."

Robert Hess: You just wrote the C# code for the class.

Mark Anders: Exactly. I can even invoke this thing. So I can go down here, it allows you to use the HTML form invocation model, and I can feed in 1+1=, and I get back an XML: 2.

Robert Hess: Well, maybe you will make some money on that, because it actually works.

Mark Anders: Well, it does work, but that's probably not the type of thing I would really expose. But I might take, for example, more complex data types, like a record set from SQL Server. I might go out, you might ask me for products of a particular category, and I might go out to SQL Server, query the database, and return them. I can very, very easily add that type of functionality. So, for example, I can import the classes that allow me to interact with data—so the data classes in the SQL Server provider. And then I can just add a method that takes an integer, which is the category, and creates a new connection to SQL Server, gives it the name of the server, does the query, and you can sort of scroll over here, SELECT * FROM product where categoryid equals the category. Then it does the query, and then just returns the data set. So, again, I'm dealing with sort of complex data type, but I don't have to think about XML and how my data type gets converted into XML.

```csharp
<%@ WebService Language="C#" Class="Demo" %>
using System;
using System.Web.Services;
using System.Data;
using System.Data.SQL;
public class Demo {
   [WebMethod]
   public int Add(int num1, int num2) {
      return num1+num2;
   }
   [WebMethod]
   public DataSet GetProducts(int category) {
      SQLConnection myConnection =
          new SQLConnection("server=localhost;uid=sa;pwd=;database=grocertogo");
      SQLDataSetCommand myCommand =
          new SQLDataSetCommand("SELECT * FROM products where categoryid="
      + category, myConnection);
      DataSet ds = new DataSet();
      myCommand.FillDataSet(ds, "Products");
      return ds;
   }
}
```

Robert Hess: There's not even any HTML in that code, either.

Mark Anders: There's no HTML, either, because it's really all about XML. So now if I come back and go to the get products method, and invoke that with dynamically— recompiled the class, and invoked that, and here's the data that got returned from SQL Server.

Robert Hess: All the XML streams, you could do with as you wish, pass it down to someone else, or whatever. So that's the way that an application programmer could take a standard programming logic that he's doing, without even doing any HTML or XML or anything like that at all: stick it on his server, expose the properties, methods, and events, using the SCL, and you as a Web programmer now could reach out and touch his Web site to see what his properties, methods, events are that he's exposing as a service, access those services, get the results back, and do whatever you want with it.

Mark Anders: And the final piece of this is that we've built this platform that enables you to build these Web applications and services. We also have the infrastructure to allow you to consume them. So from a consumer of Web services, I can naturally go out and call these things, as natural as making method calls. So again, I don't have to think about XML, I can just think about the fact that I want to invoke the "get products" Web service, and I can make a method call and get back the data, and it looks like data to me.

But finally we've created also the tools that enable you to be very productive in building these types of applications. So in Visual studio.NET, you'll be able to, just like adding references to COM components, add a reference to a Web site, a Web service, and you'll view that thing as if it was a real live object.

Robert Hess: With Auto Complete and all that stuff.

Mark Anders: Exactly, with statement completion, and it makes it very, very easy. And we've also built in things like asynchronous programming into the model, so that if you want to make sure, since you are going out over the Internet with a method call, you can do it in a very performant manner.

Robert Hess: Well, I can tell that the .NET Framework sure includes an awful lot of stuff, and I expect that we'll end up doing—we'll have to have several episodes now, talking about various aspects of the .NET Framework and C# and ASP+ and SOAP, and I hope you're willing to come back for at least one of those at some point in time to further dive into things.

Mark Anders: Yes, I definitely am. It typically takes—we just completed the PDC and we had three days of drilldown into all of this. And it's really hard to get across all of the different stuff that we've done in just 30 minutes, but the key things to take away are, number one, that we've made it simple to develop. We remove a lot of the plumbing that you have to write. Number two is with giving you a consistent programming interface to all of the different types of things that you do, whether it's building a Web application, building a Web service, accessing the event log, building a Windows application. You can move across those different domains, and you still have a very consistent view. You have the very similar design patterns, you have common collection classes, common component models, common ways that are property, or an event comes into your code. And the third thing is that we've really embodied the Internet as a programming infrastructure. Maybe embodied isn't... we've completely based the platform based on Web standards and practices where we can. So if you're building a distributed application, the way you talk from one node to another is via this Web services mechanism that uses HTTP and XML as the transport. And so it really opens up; we've provided a simple, clean, consistent way of building really scalable applications, but also that interoperate with non-Microsoft systems, so that if you're a guy running an IBM mainframe, and you want to get your data over, SOAP and HTTP are great ways to do that. IBM, for example, is doing SOAP. They've authored it with us, and submitted it to the W3C.

Robert Hess: So we're not just talking Microsoft Windows?

Mark Anders: It's not just the Microsoft standard, no. It's an open standard supported by a number of different companies. They're going to be building this into their systems as well, so it will be very easy to make different types of systems talk to each other.

Robert Hess: Which is kind of what the Web's all about, it seems like.

Mark Anders: Exactly.

Robert Hess: Well, thanks a lot, Mark. I appreciate you taking the time to share with us these demos and insights about what .NET is and show us some real code so that programmers out there in the audience can really understand what this means to them and how they can start grabbing their teeth into it. I suppose one thing that they should think about doing is trying to download that 86 MB download from the PDC release that we gave out, and playing around with that. It includes the Visual Studio 7, some of the common language runtime, the C# compiler, and some ASP+ stuff. Is that right?

Mark Anders: Well, it's a little different. The 86 MB download consists of the .NET Framework, which is all of the programming framework, so it's the common language runtime, it's ASP+, it's Windows forms, it's all of the different programming frameworks. You've got command line compilers and the SDK level stuff. It does not include Visual studio.NET. That will be released in Beta 1. This will be a preview. In some ways the most remarkable thing about the whole preview release, for me, was that, for example, the application that I was starting to build up, that's by Web site, was a site that we launched on the Internet at the PDC called ibuyspy.com, and that's www.ibuyspy.com. And it's a site that's implemented in an ASP+, and the whole .NET Framework. Being the guy who's in charge of the team that's building this, we know where it is in the whole scheme of things, it hasn't reached beta, and so where you put it on the Internet where you get thousands of hits—if it had lasted an hour, I would have said, "Well, we have some work to do, but it's kind of to be expected." But it actually lasted over 50 days, received over a million hits, and we designed the platform also to be incredibly robust and to understand that failures will happen and to be able to gracefully recover. And so after 50 days, it actually restarted itself. The server never crashed, the machine didn't have to reboot it; it just kind of migrated to a new process and kept the app running. So it's still up and running, so it's been, at this point, coming up on a couple of months.

Robert Hess: For a pre-beta, preview release of something, that sounds pretty darned good.

Mark Anders: And there are also some other sites that are on the Internet that people have already deployed with these preview bits. I think they've been having a good experience with it.

Robert Hess: Well, thanks, Mark, I appreciate you joining us. So that hopefully addressed some of the issues about programming .NET. Now as I've mentioned, future episodes are going to dive deeper into some of these capabilities, because I know we just scratched the surface. So be sure to pay attention to future episodes of the MSDN show to find out more about the .NET architecture.

The .NET Framework: Technobabble

In this transcript, Anders Hejlsberg, Distinguished Engineer at Microsoft Corporation's Developer Division, discusses the role of the .NET Framework within the overall scope and objectives of the .NET architecture. The interview was published in fall 2000 on the .NET Show on MSDN Online. Topics covered include how the .NET Framework applies to the larger vision of integrated Web services, the similarities and differences between Managed C++ and C#, how .NET dramatically simplifies the development process, the key role that runtime plays in the entire .NET story, how the .NET Framework will ultimately support all the existing versions of Windows, standardization of the framework and of C#, how all programmers will share a common set of base classes across the different languages, how the whole .NET Framework has been designed from the ground up to be object-oriented, and the availability of the framework in the real world.

Robert Hess: Welcome back. Today we're going to talk about the .NET Framework. Now if you remember the last episode, we focused on the .NET architecture. Now the framework is something slightly different, and to help us understand exactly what the .NET Framework is, and how that applies to the overall .NET vision, we have with us Anders Hejlsberg. Anders, now, you're a Distinguished Engineer at Microsoft working in the Developer Division. What exactly does that mean?

Anders Hejlsberg: Well, it means that I do a lot of sort of overall architectural work, and in this particular product cycle I worked on a new language called C# and then also as an architect for the .NET Framework

Robert Hess: Now then, C# and .NET are fairly tightly tied together, and that's where your expertise comes in.

Anders Hejlsberg: They are; .NET Framework is the overall term that we use for the .NET runtime, the .NET class libraries, and the .NET languages. C# falls in the latter category but there's also, as I said, a runtime that underlies .NET, which in a sense you can think of as the next generation of COM, and then there's a set of class libraries that provide common functionality to all the programming languages that are hosted on .NET.

Robert Hess: So when you talk about the framework and referencing it to what you are calling the runtime, to me that brings up visions of the C runtime or the VB runtime. Is it like that…?

Anders Hejlsberg: Right, right…

Robert Hess: …a physical, like, DLL that's being moved around from applications and supporting some of those sorts of capabilities. Is the same thing going on here?

Anders Hejlsberg: It's pretty much the same thing. You can think of it as, if you will, the next generation of VB run of the CRTL, if you will, except those were built for specific languages. You know VB run supports VB, and MS VCRT supports C++ and C. The .NET runtime or the .NET Framework was built from the ground up to be multilingual, meaning that you can host any programming language you care to on the runtime. We're shipping four languages in this release, or in the upcoming release: Visual Basic or VB .NET, Visual C++, C# and JScript. But we're working with external partners, commercial as well as academic, to implement a whole host of other languages ranging from APL to Cobol on the .NET Framework.

Robert Hess: And so they're accessing the runtime capabilities you're developing...

Anders Hejlsberg: Well, they're employing the runtime capabilities, if you will, such as the garbage collector exceptions, class loading, security and so forth, and they give you access to the class libraries in your applications. So you can leverage the existing set of base functionality that we give you, be that to build Web services, to build client applications, to build ASP pages, whatever.

Robert Hess: Now in the previous episode when we talked about the developing applications for .NET, we talked an awful lot about different languages, being able to develop on Cobol and C# and Visual Basic and have those different languages almost transparently call between themselves to share classes and so forth. Now, is it the runtime, then, that the framework component that's providing that infrastructure to call between the different...

Anders Hejlsberg: Yes, well, it's the framework. It's actually in a sense both the runtime and the class libraries. If you look at sort of what's happened in the world of Windows programming over time, and you—like, say we go really back to the old days where you were doing Petzold style programming. You would fire up your C compiler, #include Windows.H, you'd write your WndProcs, you'd have your WM, blah, blah, blah, Window message handlers and so forth, and you could definitely write apps that way. But it was neither easy nor particularly productive. And so what's happened over time is that we've sort of branched off from that common point and built different solutions for different scenarios, if you will. We have, for example, Visual Basic that employs principles such as delegation and composition, and RAD allows you to easily build client UI. We have MFC ATL that's sort of taken a different tack on building a more traditional class-library where you use inheritance polymorphism. It's perhaps not as productive as VB but it's more powerful. And then, most recently, we've sort of seen the birth of a whole new way of programming with ASP, with code embedded in HTML pages. One of the problems that we face because of this evolution, so to speak, is that your choice of programming model also becomes your choice of API and your choice of language. Like if you're writing an ASP page, well, you write either in VB Script or JScript and if you are accustomed to writing MFC C++ code, all your skills don't transfer, nor do the APIs that you're accustomed to, like...

Robert Hess: Because you're not going to have to create windows and message loops and...

Anders Hejlsberg: Precisely, precisely, precisely. And so what we are doing with the .NET Framework, is in a sense, we're re-unifying all of these forces, if you will. Such that we provide a consistent API that is available regardless of your programming model and your programming language. And that's really sort of one of the overarching goals for .NET...

Robert Hess: Well, I know that one of the issues with like a VB programmer, that was looking through the documentation and would find some standard Windows API function and, say, "Well, that's exactly what I get to." If that function wasn't exposed to the VB environment originally, you couldn't call it.

Anders Hejlsberg: Right.

Robert Hess: And so eventually they added some capabilities so that you could actually do call outs and redefine those functions so you could call them properly.

Anders Hejlsberg: Right. And I think that—but one thing you also see there—this is what you are talking about here is using, like, the declare statement in VB and importing entry points from DLLs. But that's really, it's not really a particularly integrated way of programming. You know you've got to declare all these function headers and it doesn't really feel natural in VB. One of the things that's very different about this upcoming release of VB is that it is a first class player in this platform. There is nothing special that you have to do to use .NET in VB to import APIs. Everything is there as a first class thing. VB, also now in this upcoming release, will support inheritance polymorphism and allow you to inherit classes from existing base classes and, indeed, you can write classes in C++, inherit from them in C# and use them in VB or any combination of those languages. It's truly multilingual and everybody's a first class player. So there are no more penalty boxes, if you will.

Robert Hess: And it's the framework, then, that is allowing VB.NET to do this?

Anders Hejlsberg: It's the runtime that allows VB.NET to do it, and it's the framework that we will all share, if you will, or the class libraries that we will all share. But, yes, the framework as an overall, yes.

Robert Hess: So, then how does the framework apply to this larger vision of integrated Web services and so forth, because a lot of time when we talk about .NET, it's always this big cloudy sort of discussion about Web services and sharing apps across stuff—where does the framework exactly fit into that model?

Anders Hejlsberg: Well, one of the things that I think characterizes the framework is that it was designed from the ground up to incorporate with Web standards and practices. It is not something that we've come in and sprinkled on as an afterthought. If you look at other ways of building applications out there, most application development tools today have roots in the client server space and really are sort of optimized for building two-tier applications, traditional client server applications, or perhaps are optimized for using an object request broker or an orb like CORBA or DCOM to do their distributed application infrastructure. From the very get-go with .NET, we realized that that sort of an architecture is not going to scale to the global scale of the Internet. One of the problems you face with say CORBA or DCOM is that those types of the serial applications tend to hold state on the server. They first of all tend to be strongly connected. You create a connection, you get a proxy object back, you're sort of holding on the client, you're holding, keeping alive some state on a server, and the problem with that is it doesn't really scale to Web forms. First of all, the quality of the connectivity over the Internet is just not good enough to do that, and second, you can't just roll in more machines and scale out, because once a client has hooked up to one server and is holding state on that server, he better stay on that server.

Anders Hejlsberg: So what we've tried to focus on is a more loosely connected stateless programming model. And instead of using proprietary protocols like IIOP or CORBA or DCOM, we're using HTTP as the carrying layer and we're using SOAP XML as the protocol over HTTP. So this gives you a number of advantages. First of all, it just works with existing firewalls. Second, it furthers this disconnected programming model because you—basically, you can shoot off an HTTP request that contains a SOAP body, invoke a Web service somewhere, it returns its result, and then there is no further record of that connection. The next time you come in, you could come in on another machine, so you can scale it out. You can use sort of the Web practices that we use for scaling of your applications, yet you can get a view of the world that looks like objects and classes and methods, and so forth.

Robert Hess: Now, with all this talk about applications and SOAP and XML and HTTP requests, and stuff like that, if I was designing an application that wasn't going across the Internet—it was just staying on my local machine—does that mean I can't use .NET for that?

Anders Hejlsberg: No, no, absolutely not. What I'm saying is just that if you are building distributed applications, we give you this great infrastructure in place. And it actually ties in nicely even with apps that are not distributed. That doesn't necessarily mean that you have no need for XML. And our XML parser is not specifically tied to doing SOAP; it's a general XML parser. And also, of course, the framework includes support for writing traditional client applications, for writing Web server back ends, or for writing just computational applications that do file IO, for example.

Robert Hess: So, what if I had, like, a Legacy application, existing application based on big database querying service sort of thing that I was putting out on my Windows system. Maybe it was running across the internal network using very tight coupled network connections across there. How would I take advantage of the .NET Framework and environment in this existing application?

Anders Hejlsberg: Well, I think what you would do is you would in a sense stay with the same architecture that you have; you would evolve in a sense. First of all, we don't really believe in throwing away your existing code, and rather, we focused heavily on giving you ways to interop and to evolve your existing code...

Robert Hess: So I wouldn't have to rewrite in C#?

Anders Hejlsberg: You would not have to rewrite in C#. And say you're writing in C++, for example; well, you would use Managed C++ and we have, in fact...

Robert Hess: So I've got to rewrite it into Managed C++, right?

Anders Hejlsberg: No you do not. All you have to do is throw a switch on the compiler and it's the "it just works" switch.

Robert Hess: Yeah, I've heard that before...

Anders Hejlsberg: That's it.

Robert Hess: I mean...really, if I've got code, I don't have to go into, "Oh, but you called your pointers wrong or you did this wrong." I can take existing code and just throw a switch on it and for the most part, it should just compile?

Anders Hejlsberg: Yes. Yes, that's precisely what the design goal of that feature is. You throw the switch on the compiler; instead of compiling to traditional unmanaged code, we now compile your application to managed code. Now, of course, that doesn't mean that you automatically get garbage collection of your objects because C++ is fundamentally not a garbage collected language. But it gives you a lot of the other features of the .NET Framework such as deployment and security, plus it gives you great interoperability with the .NET Framework so you can write these hybrid applications that do a bunch of traditional stuff using traditional C++ classes, yet also use managed or garbage collected classes from the .NET Framework.

Robert Hess: In the last episode, Mark Anders showed us some sample code—where he said, "Here's the standard C++ way of registering events in the Event Log and putting a bunch of events into it," and it was standard MSDN code you got online; it was like two dozen, three dozen lines of code—looked pretty ugly, really. And then he showed the C# .NET version of that, which was like, four lines of code. So let's say I've got this Legacy application. I decide that I need to take and do something in the Event Log because I know it's important but this code is ugly. I want to use this C# code. What would I have to do to take and use those four lines of code? Could I include them in my Managed C++ code or would I want to call something outside written as a C# thing, or does it matter?

Anders Hejlsberg: Well, you could do either. First of all, Managed C++ and C# are, in a sense, very similar when it comes to using managed objects. It's the same syntax—object.methodName(arguments), for example. It's the same syntax to instantiate objects; you use the new operator and so forth. The thing that Managed C++ gives you is the ability, in a sense, to write both code that targets traditional C++ classes and code that targets the new garbage collector class model in the .NET Framework within that same method. You can mix and match even within the same expressions, if you will. And of course, that code could be using a class that was written in C# because once you're using the .NET Framework, any language can consume any other language's API...

Robert Hess: ...The framework's just making that transparent...

Anders Hejlsberg: ...Yes, that completely...

Robert Hess: ...So then...

Anders Hejlsberg: Now one thing I actually wanted to add to this, as well, is—and you mentioned how the traditional C++ way was umpteen lines of code, and in C# it was only four lines of code—I think that speaks to one other thing that we really focused very hard on, which is to dramatically simplify the development process, to enable the programmer to think about his algorithms instead of thinking about housekeeping. One of the things that really plagued COM over time is this incredible amount of GUID, HResult, AddRef / Release, coCreateInstance; put stuff in the Registry, and so forth, and you know your code just explodes into this macro mumble jumble that you can't read it; it's write-only code.

Robert Hess: Which is why ATL came out to make that a little bit easier for you.

Anders Hejlsberg: Sure, sure. But even ATL is still not for the uninitiated, I would say, and then we really focused hard on making all of that housekeeping go away. There are no more GUIDs, there are no more HResults, there's no AddRef / Release, there's no coCreateInstance; it's all gone. Gone. And basically it's replaced with intimate knowledge in the language of the underlying runtime.

Robert Hess: So then the runtime really is an extremely important part of the entire .NET story.

Anders Hejlsberg: Absolutely.

Robert Hess: It sounds like that that's the thing that makes everything work properly.

Anders Hejlsberg: Yes, yes, it's sort of this ephemeral thing. You never really see it or physically interact with it. It's just there but it provides a whole host of very important services to apps that run under the .NET Framework. One thing that comes to mind, of course, is garbage collection and another is exception handling, code verification, class loading, threading model, et cetera, et cetera. All of these sort of black boxes, this machinery, is part of the .NET Framework. It's shared across all applications so everybody can leverage it and interoperate much better.

Robert Hess: Now, so the framework then is binary code, like maybe a DLL or something like that, that's going to be running the system. That means that it's got to be written for Windows NT, Windows 2000, Windows 98, Windows 95. Which versions of Windows is it going to be supported on?

Anders Hejlsberg: Well, the framework will support all of those. Currently, the current alpha release that we have out right now only allows you to develop on Windows 2000, simply because we're just trying to reduce the bug reporting matrix. The final product will support Windows 95, 98, NT 4, and Windows 2000. So all of our, and indeed the compact, framework will target Windows CE. So we will have broad support in the .NET Framework for all of the versions of Windows that we have out there.

Robert Hess: Now, and then I'm assuming that the framework then is going to be an important component of Windows operating systems all moving forward, and integrating it deeper and deeper so that Windows and the applications that come with Windows will automatically just be .NET applications as well.

Anders Hejlsberg: Right. Well, I mean, eventually the .NET Framework will simply be a part of Windows just like kernel 32.DLL is part of it. Well, so will these DLLs be part of it and it will be ephemeral.

Robert Hess: Then, with the Internet being a set of systems that allow different computers to talk to each other pretty well, and I'm on a Windows system and I'm calling a .NET Framework API sort of thing, and I'm calling across the Net to some other system like a Macintosh or a Linux machine or something like that, am I going to have a breakdown there if I'm not running .NET over those other systems?

Anders Hejlsberg: No, you're not. That is the—this goes back to what I was talking about earlier, that for any kind of distributed system, we are actually not requiring .NET to be present. As I said, we use HTTP as a carrying layer, use XML SOAP for the package and protocol. And, indeed, when you develop Web services with the .NET Framework, we give you all the infrastructure that's required, not just to actually implement the service but also to describe using XML, the schema of your Web service, if you will. What are the methods that are available in my Web service; what arguments do they take? What are the function results? Those things go into SCL files, which is a particular kind of XML...

Robert Hess: ...Yeah, we talked a little bit in the last episode...

Anders Hejlsberg: Right, right. And the data types are described by XSD which is the W3C standard for describing data types, if you will. All of that infrastructure we give you in the .NET Framework. In fact, if you think about, when I describe this to programmers, I try to sort of relate it to what a programmer knows in terms of concepts. And programmers kind of know things like objects, they know classes, they know methods. They know about making calls to methods. And for all of those things there are actually standards, either existing standards or emerging standards, on the Web. For objects or for data, well, there's a standard called XML that allows you describe any piece of data and transport it, and we provide you a bi-directional mapping between objects and XML, or XML and objects in the .NET Framework, completely transparently.

Robert Hess: And so the object is being re-emitted as an XML stream?

Anders Hejlsberg: It can be serialized as XML transported over a distributed system or just stored for future retrieval. And then you can retrieve it and reconstitute the object from that XML...

Robert Hess: So it would be similar—like current applications—if they want to take and save their current memory state, for instance...just kind of point to the head pointer and say, "This and the next 300 bytes are all part of my state; save that to disk and read back..."

Anders Hejlsberg: Yes. You don't actually say the next 300 bytes, but yes, precisely that actually is in the framework and it's called serialization. We support pluggable formatters. One being a binary formatter which is useful if you're just marshalling objects between two processes or two threads, you really don't care about turning them into XML and then immediately turning them back into objects. You just want to like, get it over the wire as fast as possible and so you would use the binary formatter. But we also have an XML formatter that allows you to turn it into XML and, indeed, even adhere to a particular XML schema because...

Robert Hess: ...Like a BizTalk schema...

Anders Hejlsberg: Exactly. Exactly, yes. Yes.

Robert Hess: Now, okay, so let's say we've got the notion of "I've got my .NET runtime based application running on Windows and I'm talking to some other server, Linux or whatever." Now, let's say I'm a programmer and I'm working in a multi-platform environment and I want to take advantage of some of these .NET capabilities. Does .NET itself run on Linux? Run on the Macintosh and stuff like that?

Anders Hejlsberg: It does not, currently. It is designed to be technically possible to run it on the Linux, but we're not making any commitments one way or the other at this point in time. What we are doing, though, is we are submitting the .NET Framework, or rather, what we call the common language infrastructure, to ECMA for standardization, and that basically is a subset of the .NET Framework that we expect to be standardized with working partners. We're also submitting C#, the programming language, to the same standardization committee and we're hoping to kick this effort off in fact this month. And, of course, that will inevitably, down the line, lead to implementations on different operating systems such as the Mac OS and certainly such as UNIX and such as Linux.

Robert Hess: So the difference there would be that, say that Apple decided that this .NET thing really works very well, Apple could take and develop the .NET Framework for the Macintosh because they...

Anders Hejlsberg: Well, they probably wouldn't call it the .NET Framework but there would be a standard for a .NET-like runtime called the common language infrastructure; ECMA would have to name it. You know we would adhere to that standard. Apple's implementation would adhere to that standard. A Linux implementation would adhere to that standard.

Robert Hess: And the sort of things that a programmer working with that would expect is the garbage collection models and the abilities to call between applications...

Anders Hejlsberg: Precisely, and a certain set of base classes that you can expect to find present on each platform. Now of course, as you go down to smaller devices, this will have to be a layered cake, right. On a small device you're not going to want to carry around, say, interfaces to a database, because there may not be one on this small device. But we will layer this, work with ECMA and our partners to layer this such that you can sort of cut it off at an appropriate level.

Robert Hess: So then if the .NET Framework is designed with this concept of being available on different platforms, perhaps if someone else wanted to port it across, does that also mean you designed for a—like a lowest common denominator approach so you don't really have full access to the hardware you're currently running on?

Anders Hejlsberg: No, no, not at all. I mean, the implementations of the .NET Framework will take advantage of whatever is available on the platform that they're implemented on. Of course if you're implemented on a small device, there's limited stuff to take advantage of...

Robert Hess: Like on a coffee cup...

Anders Hejlsberg: Yes, precisely, on your refrigerator. However, if you are on, say, a multi-processor machine, a heavy, high end box, we in fact have different implementations of the garbage collector: one for single processor machines, one for MP machines, and on a multi-processor machine, we will actually tune for that environment. The garbage collector will actually divvy memory up to four different arenas that each processor, each thread on each processor, will allocate memory from a different arena, yet the garbage collector will sort of orchestrate and collect across all four processors. But that sort of an implementation reduces contention, gives you much higher throughput, and we see that in our scaling benchmarks, too, that we really, really scale well on MP boxes.

Robert Hess: I guess the issue there is it's like, as a programmer running an application, accessing the .NET Framework, I'm not specifically using the .NET Framework to get to a feature of the current hardware I'm running on. The .NET Framework is providing these services and I'm just simply utilizing that...

Anders Hejlsberg: Precisely, and that's precisely why it's important to have a set of base class libraries that in a sense abstract underlying services from the operating system such as IO.

Robert Hess: Now to probably try to draw everything together here, we've talked about a lot of different topics in talking about this .NET Framework, which is a fairly identifiable component of the whole .NET architecture. What exactly do you think are the key aspects of the .NET Framework that our audience needs to understand?

Anders Hejlsberg: Okay, well, I think first of all it is the fact that it dramatically simplifies your application development. As I talked about before, all of this housekeeping that you traditionally have to deal with when you're writing COM applications, it's just gone. A whole class of bugs have been eliminated by the introduction of the garbage collector; error handling is going to be more robust because we use exceptions instead of H results. Your code is going to be type safe, at least if you're writing in VB or C#, in the sense that you will not have any uninitialized variables. It's impossible to have them. It is impossible to make an unsafe type cast.

Robert Hess: Now is that coming from the .NET Framework, or is that coming from like C# or...

Anders Hejlsberg: It's in a sense coming from both. The .NET Framework provides a definition of an instruction language that we call MSIL, for Microsoft Intermediate Language. Our compilers target that intermediate language. So when you compile source code in, say, C#, we're actually not producing X86 object code. Rather we're producing MSIL, which then gets compiled at runtime by a JID compiler, or at install time by the install time JID, into native code on whatever CPU you are using. So...

Robert Hess: So that intermediate code model that is supporting the initialized variables and the type safe things...

Anders Hejlsberg: Well, that—so the IL in a sense gives you a base level, then, upon which you can build features such as code verification that verifies that your code adheres to certain rules and therefore is type safe. That's very hard to do with an X86 code. You look at some X86 code and you really have no idea what it's going to do and whether it's going to be safe, whether it is never going to use a pointer that is no longer allocated, whether it's going to overrun the end of an array, whether it's going to access an uninitialized variable. It's literally impossible to see that from X86 code. But it is possible to verify that. To verify the IL. Indeed there is a verifiable subset of the IL that the runtime will permit to run in a less trusted environment than, for example, code that you have permanently and physically installed on your machine will have a high degree of trust. The code you that you download over the Internet will have a low degree of trust and will be subject to verification. So there's all these infrastructures in place that actually allows you to write robust code that can be transported over the Net...

Robert Hess: That's separate from the compiler itself.

Anders Hejlsberg: It's separate; it's shared by all of the compilers, if you will.

Anders Hejlsberg: Now, in the compiler, though, just to sort of round it out on the C# side at least, there's a core part of the C# language that's type safe. But we also support a feature called unsafe code in C# that allows you to say, "Hey, I need you to turn off this verification thing here." Now, I am willing to accept the fact that this code cannot be downloaded over the Internet, or at least not without the use of granting it more trust than it would get by default. However, having accepted that, I am now permitted to operate on pointers and do things that in the end are not type safe. Because ultimately, the rubber has to meet the road, and when you're interoperating with existing APIs that are not type safe, you have to have that bridging layer.

Robert Hess: That also then brings into notion that, of these DLLs that aren't type safe causing the problems and so forth—you're probably better off if you can stay within...

Anders Hejlsberg: Absolutely, and, indeed, like I said, code that gets downloaded, you have to stay within that subset, yes.

Robert Hess: So then it sounds to me that one of the important aspects of the framework is this whole IL model that is enforcing this type safety, which will greatly reduce some of the problems people experience today with their applications?

Anders Hejlsberg: Well, the IL thing does many things. First of all, of course, it frees you from a particular CPU architecture because if you have a just-in-time compiler, well, it will compile it to the right CPU, whatever you're running on. But, as I said, the other important aspect of IL is the notion that you can actually implement a security system. You can't really implement a security system on top of just raw X86 code.

Robert Hess: Because you don't know what the structure is at all.

Anders Hejlsberg: Exactly, yes.

Robert Hess: So what other aspects of the framework do you think are important that people need to understand to really understand how to incorporate their applications in this whole .NET environment?

Anders Hejlsberg: Well, I think that as I talked about before, first of all, it's the notion that we now all share a common set of base classes across the different languages, across the different programming models. Whether you're writing a client application that's just going to bring up traditional client windows or whether you're writing ASP code that goes on the back end of your Web server, the same APIs are available. You know the way you would do file IO. It's precisely the same and it doesn't matter what language you're in and what kind of application you're writing. That is very important. I think, also, the whole framework has been designed from the ground up to be object oriented, if you will. So there—now we are broadly making available the notion of polymorphism inheritance and in that way, in a sense deriving from a starting point instead of implementing from scratch. That, of course, has been available in some of our framework so far, again, in C and ATL, but it has, for example, not really been available in VB, and certainly not in when you're writing a Web page.

Robert Hess: Well, thank you. I mean, I hope that we've answered some of our audience's questions that they might have on the framework. I know that it seems like a really big topic to cover. The overview we covered in the last episode just glossed over an awful lot of stuff and gave a good overview. Here, we've tried to dive into what one aspect is: the framework. Now, I'm hoping that you will be available for the next episode, which I'm planning on covering with C#. And I understand you've got a pretty deep understanding of the C# issue.

Anders Hejlsberg: Yes, that was part of designing it, and so definitely. And I would certainly also urge people to grab the framework, download it, and play with it, and actually feel for yourself what I'm talking about.

Robert Hess: Now, on actually playing with it, brings up one final question: what's the availability expected to be of this in the real world?

Anders Hejlsberg: Well, currently, an alpha version of the framework is available for...broadly for downloads. No restrictions.

Robert Hess: And I included information in the last episode on how to get that. At the bottom of the transcript I'll put another link down with that stuff.

Anders Hejlsberg: Okay, great. We are currently working on Beta I, which is slated to come out fairly soon. There will then be a Beta II, and then finally RTM sometime next year as part of Visual Studio.NET.

Robert Hess: So then, as early as a year from now, people will actually be able to sell applications that are using the .NET Framework and .NET architecture.

Anders Hejlsberg: Right, but surprisingly, or wonderfully, I should say, we are actually seeing people deploy Web sites already built, using ASP+, C#, VB on the Net—real world Web sites.

Robert Hess: On a pre-alpha release.

Anders Hejlsberg: Yes.

Robert Hess: Well, that's pretty exciting.

Anders Hejlsberg: Yeah, we're pretty excited about it.

Robert Hess: Well, thanks, Anders. Thanks for joining us for this architecture section talking about the .NET Framework. After this brief break we'll come back and talk to you about the programming issues that programmers need to understand to program for the .NET Framework. So join us for that.

The .NET Framework: Enter the Programmer

In this transcript, Brian Harry, Product Unit Manager for Common Language Runtime, discusses programming within the .NET parameters. The interview was published in fall 2000 on the .NET Show on MSDN Online. Topics covered include what it means to use the .NET Framework, the richness of the class library for the .NET Framework, the extent to which the framework is tool-friendly, the functionality of the class library, the fact that the .NET Framework supports and requires self-describing components, and the key things that application developers need to understand about the advantages that the .NET Framework provides them.

Robert Hess: Welcome back. Now as I mentioned earlier, today we're talking about a .NET Framework. Now Anders took and talked a lot about some of the high level issues with the architecture and what that means to the different programming models, and the different languages we might use. But actually programming to the .NET parameters and understanding what that means from a structure standpoint of the code you add to your applications, and how you can take existing applications and move those forward, is extremely important for all of you, I'm sure. So, to understand that better, I have with me Brian Harry. Brian Harry is a Product Unit Manager for the Common Language Runtime.

Brian Harry: That is correct.

Robert Hess: And you've got some input and ideas on exactly what it means to use the .NET Framework and applications and such.

Brian Harry: Absolutely.

Robert Hess: So now, at the PDC, we took and first showed people what the .NET Framework was, and I guess a lot of the people have actually been having a lot of fun doing some coding with the bits we handed them, plus there is that big download you can download from our Web site to download some of the class libraries and .NET functionality. What exactly are people touching then in code when they're actually writing applications? What does it mean to use the .NET Framework? What do they see?

Brian Harry: Okay. Well, the .NET Framework is a very broad set of things. It includes a runtime environment, the Common Language Runtime, and it includes a set of class libraries that you can use. Within those class libraries, there are a set of application models. There's the WinForms application model, which is for building sort of the traditional Windows GUI apps that people are used to, with forms and buttons and things like that. There's the WebForms programming model, which provides a framework or class libraries for building Web applications that includes basic ability to render HTML. There's a data access ability for doing SQL queries and for taking the data returned from SQL and very quickly and easily turning it into XML or turning it into HTML that can then be projected to the client to create a UI.

Robert Hess: So then to probably oversimplify that a bit, and I'm probably going to be stepping on toes here, but the WinForms is kind of like Visual Basic and the WebForms is kind of like Front Page?

Brian Harry: I wouldn't quite say that. Our goal has been to take the Visual Basic ease of use and very simple RAD application development and continue to provide that for rich client apps which we've had for a long time, and to take that same basic experience and provide it for Web applications. So, when you're designing a Web page, it's very, very much like designing an existing form in Windows. I have a canvas that I work on, which is the Web page, and using Visual Studio, I can drag and drop controls, and when I've got the controls I want, I can very simply double-click on the control and go into the event that I want to edit to put some code behind that form. So that's really the kind of design environment we're going for for the Web as well.

Robert Hess: So not two different environments, but one environment that can either go either one way or the other.

Brian Harry: That's correct. I would say a very similar developer experience for both application models. Now, of course, there are differences in the application models. The Web application model is a loosely coupled, disconnected, generally low trust between client and server application model, and you have to worry about authentication and a bunch of those problems, and usually you're projecting HTML. And the Windows application model, of course, is a tightly coupled, somewhere underneath is a Windows message pump, pumping messages. So, at a plumbing level they're very different, but we're trying to make it so that from a developer experience you're ultimately doing a lot of similar things. You're interacting with the user, you're presenting some UI, the user is entering data, he's pushing buttons, and we want to make a lot of that sort of very similar, very familiar to developers.

Robert Hess: That sounds kind of like some of the original intents behind Visual Basic, was to take and create "forget about the message loop, forget about create window, forget about some other stuff; let's just draw things on the screen and make them work properly."

Brian Harry: That's correct.

Robert Hess: I know that from my own experience in using VB, there were times where I would kind of run into this wall, that "Okay, I can't go any further. I'm needing access to this thing that I know about in this other API set, but I can't access it." How rich is the class library for the .NET Framework?

Brian Harry: Well, the class library for the .NET Framework is very rich. It's very large. There are a lot of classes in it. Further, there is another very important design principle of the .NET Framework, which is we are very familiar with sort of the VB experience of what we sort of think of us falling off the cliff of, "If I want to do what it does for me, then everything is great. But I want to sort of do it slightly differently, I want to tweak the behavior a little bit, it becomes pretty hard and very frequently I just sort of have to go back to the WIN 32 API and roll it on my own." One of the key design principles of the .NET Framework is it's an object oriented, inheritance based system. So part of what we had to do is we added inheritance to VB in order to do this. Of course, C++ already has inheritance and C#, being a C++ like language, also has inheritance. And we make use of that very heavily in our framework, where we sort of go from a very simple abstraction to increasingly richer abstractions through multiple levels, and I'm able to tie in and override behavior and call functions at each level of that hierarchy. So I don't have—I can use the most derived level, and sort of generally the easiest and the simplest, and it gives me the 80% case of what people want, but then if I want to do something slightly differently, I can just go up one level of abstraction in the hierarchy and work there without having to sort of start from scratch and build from the beginning.

Robert Hess: So the class libraries are trying to encompass everything an application might need access to.

Brian Harry: Certainly that's our eventual goal. I'm not going to say that in V1 we're doing everything that an application would ever want to do. But eventually, the goal is to provide a comprehensive, very easy-to-use class library to solve the problems that programmers need solved. Another goal that I wanted to bring out is that we have worked very hard to make this framework very tool friendly, so that we make sort of that VB RAD design time behavior easy for a tool to implement, and our Visual Studio Tool has done a fabulous job building on top of that. That's been a great tool.

Robert Hess: So that making it more tool friendly, is that part of the framework and this minimum language support model you were talking about?

Brian Harry: The Common Language Runtime.

Robert Hess: The Common Language Runtime. So those two things work together and the C# thing, too? Or is that...

Brian Harry: Absolutely, absolutely. Really, the tool friendliness has to be baked in from the bottom up into every component. There is fundamental support within the Common Language Runtime, like the notion of attributes. There's support within the languages for letting the user expose attributes, for parsing code for the designers, for parsing and formatting code, and then there's the Visual Studio aspect of the actual designer support that allows me to drag and drop things and view the properties, et cetera.

Robert Hess: So if I was a compiler writer and I was currently working on a Modular II or a Fortran compiler or something like that, and I was following all the guidelines for integrating well with the .NET Framework, should be fairly easy then for me to add some sort of tool-like model like that to it?

Brian Harry: Yes, absolutely. We've set out a bunch of conventions that people can use in order to get that kind of behavior.

Robert Hess: Now, I guess also if I was a compiler vendor, I might want to take and add just my language to the Visual Studio product. Is that something that's being supported as well, or is that just for later revs?

Brian Harry: We have the Visual Studio Integrators Program that we are encouraging third parties to join, and this allows them to tie into the Visual Studio environment. So absolutely.

Robert Hess: Okay. What sort of functional stuff does the class library contain? How deep does it go?

Brian Harry: Well, let me show you. We've got this internal tool we have here called Meteor which basically takes all of our class libraries and processes them just to produce HTML pages off of it, and one of the things, as I show you this, you need to understand is the—our class libraries are broken down into a set of namespaces, like C++ namespaces that sort of encapsulate functionality. So we've got a set of namespaces for the rich Windows application. We've got a set of namespaces for the Web application model. We've got a set of namespaces for data access. We've got some things that we call the base class library, which is sort of the lowest level of functionality. So what you can see here is a pretty long list of namespaces. These are top level namespaces within the product. Let's just drill down into one just to see what—how much stuff is in these namespaces. Let's look, for example, at WinForms, which is the namespace for creating rich Windows client applications. Within a namespace is a bunch of classes, and I'll just page through them so you can kind of get an idea of how much there is.

Robert Hess: Now I assume this list is actually being generated dynamically by enumerating through the class libraries.

Brian Harry: That's correct. We've got a tool that processes through the actual DLLs that we ship, and produces this stuff. One of the important things to understand about the .NET Framework is all the components are self-describing. This is an incredibly important feature that we use to give sort of very rich development experience, and also to give some very good deployment capabilities to simplify a bunch of the deployment problems that people face today. For example, every component describes both what is in it, what classes are in it, and what it depends on. So, if you've got problems loading an application, you can go find out what it depends on, say, "Oh, I'm missing that DLL", and makes it a lot easier to manage our application. And I can keep going. This is just the rich Windows, and as you can see, it's hundreds and hundreds of classes in the rich Windows model. So let's pick one of these just to drill down into and I'll give you an idea of how much stuff you can find in a class. Let's take the FileDialog class, which is sort of a wrapper for the standard Windows common control file dialog, and it will have a set of methods, things like OnFileOk, which is an event that's fired when the user hits the OKAY button on the file dialog, and a set of properties for setting whether the dialog's going to check if the file exists, if the path exists, et cetera.

Robert Hess: And so you set those just like you set properties and script code or something like that.

Brian Harry: Absolutely. Many of them can be set in the Design Time environment. In Visual Studio there's a little Properties dialog which I'll show you in a bit, where you can just click the values of the properties, or they can be set in code for what you'd like to do. Let's pick—let me shut down the WinForms one here and I'll go for a minute into something else, just to go into a completely different area of the framework, give you an idea of how broad it is. Let's look for example at System.IO. Everybody needs to do file IO and network IO, et cetera. System.IO has a set of the base primitives for IO. It's got definitions of stream classes, it's got a definition of a file, and file and directory classes. So, for example, the File class has all you would need to copy files, to create files, delete them...

Robert Hess: Now one thing I'm noticing here is like this Delete function. You say it takes a string parameter into it and it even tells me that string parameter is the path.

```
Pub s Void Delete (String path)
```

Brian Harry: That's correct.

Robert Hess: So it's documenting what type of information it's expecting there, and so that's all part of when you wrote the Delete function the way you described it in code, self-documented...

Brian Harry: That's exactly correct. So that sort of feeds back into what I was saying a minute ago about the—one of the key aspects is that the .NET Framework supports self-describing components, in fact, requires self-describing components. So not only does it tell you what's in there and what it depends on, but it also tells you how to use what's in there. It tells you all the parameters and their types, and I'll show you some very cool features in Visual Studio and how it uses that information to make the developer experience absolutely wonderful.

Robert Hess: I remember in the early days of the releases of many other operating systems and things, one of the problems developers would have in the alpha and beta stages is when the function built into the operating system didn't match the documentation...

Brian Harry: Right.

Robert Hess: Because things had changed between writing the documentation and actually implementing the function. And so this makes that impossible to happen, then.

Brian Harry: Yeah, it does. It makes it a lot less frequent that you have to go back to Help, because the information, as I said—I'll show you in Visual Studio—the information is just there as you type. Visual Studio is reading that metadata that describes the functions and it's prompting you with telling you what the parameters are and what their types are.

Robert Hess: Now, since this is part of the way C# and the .NET Framework and the other languages that participate in this works—this means if I was an application developer at Boeing or something like that and I was writing my applications, my components and so forth, this would also be documenting what I was writing, too?

Brian Harry: That's correct.

Robert Hess: And so my components could now be exposed to the other users in my group that might be using it in the same fashion.

Brian Harry: That's correct.

Robert Hess: Oh, that's exciting.

Brian Harry: So, let me just sort of hit a couple other areas in the framework again, just to give you a flavor of what all is in here. There's the System.Data and System.Data.ADO, which is all of our data access which supports both connected and disconnected data access model. Again, I'll just click on this briefly and show you, again, lots of classes that provide all the different functionality of databases. Another point that I'd like to make is that our data access is very integrated with our XML. We view this as a huge advantage of the .NET Framework of allowing you to view the same data either as an XML tree or as relational data, and to be able to transform that data back and forth as necessary. We think this is a very valuable feature, especially in Web based programming, where what you're generally exchanging over the wire is XML, and then you want to manipulate it with relational tools both on the server and on the client. A couple other things I just want to point out: for example, we've got System.ComServices is in here, which is our wrapper for the...I'm sorry, Microsoft.ComServices, which is our wrapper for the existing Win32 COM+ functionality, which gives you automatic transactions and object pooling and queuing and features like that. We've got a bunch of compiler support classes like System.CodeDOM, which allows—it's just an interface for parsing code for designers.

Robert Hess: I'm noticing these Microsoft Dot classes...

Brian Harry: Yes...

Robert Hess: I'm assuming that means these are specific technologies that are Microsoft technology putting in there. Does this also then mean that other companies that have technologies, if they want to add to this system, they'd have their company name in front of them?

Brian Harry: That's correct. So the way the naming convention is—quite honestly, it's not particularly enforced—is that the system namespace is sort of for generic system functionality...

Robert Hess: Like file IO...

Brian Harry: Like file IO, like database access, like GUI, like some basic Web APIs, and then for Microsoft-specific functionality or company-specific functionality that's designed to go in a namespace that starts with the company name. So we have a bunch of Microsoft namespace things, and then most of the stuff that we've done to date has been in sort of the category of basic system services.

Robert Hess: So if I installed, let's say, AppleTalk drivers to my system, that were written in that framework, it would say Apple.NETworking.AppleTalk or something like that?

Brian Harry: Yes. Yes. So, I think that probably covers most of it. We could spend hours just going through all the different support here. There's a broad set of Web namespaces that handle security, that handle the UI, that handle support for what we call Web Services. There's been a lot of talk about Web Services lately; the basic notion is this notion of cooperating components across the Web where I can make a function call, have that turn into an XML message, deliver that to a server across the Internet, have it process that XML message and return a value, and have that turned back into XML and returned back to me...

Robert Hess: Your application need not realize you're doing XML in the stream.

Brian Harry: That's correct. And we abstract that away from the user having to deal with—with a lot of flexibility for creating the schema that you want out of your parameters, because ultimately the schema is what matters on the wire, a very powerful programming model for really taking the Web to the next generation. The Web has been so much about a server projecting HTML, and Web Service is about a collaborative Web environment where servers are working together and clients are working together independent of presentation, but instead exchanging data that can be processed independently to create rich local interfaces, to aggregate services across Web servers, et cetera.

Robert Hess: So from a programmer's standpoint, actually using some of this great class library functionality like this, what is their experience like and how can they actually make use of these things?

Brian Harry: Okay, well, let me do a little demo for you in Visual Studio, and I've chosen to do a WinForms demo. I could have just as easily have done a WebForms demo or some data access...

Robert Hess: So essentially you're going to be writing a traditional Windows application.

Brian Harry: That's right.

Robert Hess: Right.

Brian Harry: So this is Visual Studio 7 or VS.NET. If you went to the PDC then you have a version of this.

Robert Hess: But this is not—this was at the PDC...

Brian Harry: That's correct.

Robert Hess: This is not part of the download...

Brian Harry: That's correct...

Robert Hess: That you get off the Web site.

Brian Harry: Visual Studio is not part of the download. It was handed out at the PDC. It will be available again when we do a beta later this year. Most everything I'm going to show you—in fact, I'd say everything I'm going to show you—you can do purely with the SDK. You just don't get the really rich and nice design environment that we have here in Visual Studio.

Robert Hess: That's just another reason to go to the PDC.

Brian Harry: So I've just created a new WinForms project. Now it's going to come up. It comes up in a default view with an empty form very much like VB would do for me to now work on. So, let's just create a very simple form as to illustrate some of the basic principles. And notice I can—very VB-like, just I have this toolbox over here and I can drag and drop controls and I can resize them as necessary. Just keep dragging them on here. Let's throw in a couple of buttons and another button. Make it look a little bit pretty for you. And then we'll add a ListBox. And I'm not going to make it look perfect but...there you go. And I mentioned earlier about how a lot of the properties can be set inside Visual Studio and you don't have to—you can set them in code or in the Visual Studio. So, let's take, for example, the button, and I want to change the text of this button to "Add." So I can click over here on this property grid, which is context dependent; depending on what control I click on, different properties show up. So I will change the text of that button to "Add."

Robert Hess: Just to clarify, in the earlier demo we were looking at the Meteor demo. We saw System.WinForms. Blah de blah...

Brian Harry: That's correct...

Robert Hess: What you just clicked on there was System.WinForms.button.

Brian Harry: That's correct.

Robert Hess: And in the same way that in your Window view you were seeing all the property events exposed by "button," this is just showing you down here in the Properties dialog those properties.

Brian Harry: That's correct. This is showing you the properties. There is another tab here that will let you see the events. The methods don't show up here because there's no design support for the methods. That's for you to code to. So I'll change the name of this one to "Delete," and last thing I'll do, just for the heck of it, is change—is remove the text out of this TextBox. So here we have a button, or a dialog with text in a button and some buttons on it, and what I'm going to do is now write some code behind this form. So, what I'd like to do is whenever I type in this TextBox, I'd like to change the enabled or disabled state of the "Add" button. And, ultimately, what I'm imagining I'd do with this is write something that I would type, and add things to the—add what I type to the ListBox. So all I have to do is double click on it and that's going to take me out of the designer and into the code. So before we actually go and write the code for this, let me just show you a little bit around this source file. So everything I just did is represented in this source file. The designer—what it actually does, it doesn't create sort of the Win32 resources that we're used to, which is a declarative view of your form. Instead, it generates code. So what that means is, all of that code is available for you to modify and tweak any way you want. It also means you don't have to have the designer to do anything. It's all there in code. So one of the key aspects for WinForms is this function called "InitializedComponent()". InitializedComponent is where most of what I did in that designer actually shows up.

```
private void InitializeComponent()
{
    this.components = new System.ComponentModel.Container ();
    this.textBox1 = new System.WinForms.TextBox();
    this.button1 = new System.WinForms.Button ();
    this.label1 = new System.WinForms.Label ();
    this.listBox1 = new System.WinForms.ListBox ();
    this.button2 = new System.WinForms.Button ();
```

... and a bunch more stuff, but you really don't need to see this, do you?

It has generated all the code to create each of the controls, so you will see a new of System.WinForms.TextBox and Button and Label and ListBox and another Button. And then you'll see all the property settings. Now, a bunch of these were set by default. Only a few of them did I actually tweak.

Robert Hess: So here's like that button.Text = "Add."

```
button1.Text = "Add";
```

Brian Harry: That's correct.

Robert Hess: That's where you clicked on that box and you said "Add" and that changed the value here.

Brian Harry: That's exactly right, and button.Text equals "Delete," and it's automatically put in all of the properties for the location and the size and the tab index and all of that. Now this can actually, for a fairly complicated form, this can get pretty complicated. It can get to be a pretty long function. And you don't always want to be paging up and down over that. So I want to show you a neat feature of Visual Studio. They've added an outlining mode where I can just collapse that whole function, and that turns into a plus and it's got this little dot-dot-dot out here that lets you know that there's some more code behind there. And now I don't have to see that code generated by the designer. But I always can go and modify it if I want, and in fact I believe that in Visual Basic projects, that will be the default. You will not see the code that the designer has generated.

Robert Hess: Oh, because they're not used to seeing the code. Because that's how you used to use a separate form for all that.

Brian Harry: That's correct, they've never seen it before and we don't want to change that experience for the VB developer. So let's write a little code. And let's say that, again, what I said I wanted to do was make it so that as I—the enabled state of the "Add" button changes based on whether I have typed any text or not. So let's start by—since I haven't—when I pulled up the form I haven't typed any text. Let's start by setting that to Disabled. So we'll just simply type button1.—and you'll notice this pop-up just came up, as I was typing; essentially it happens as soon as I hit dot, it says, "Ah, he's going to type another member here." It knows that I've just typed button1 and it knows what button1 is. It knows it's a button. So it goes into that DLL, the WinForms DLL, and says, "Okay, show me the methods and properties of buttons so that I can present those to the user."

And you'll notice, also, as I type, it sort of incrementally goes to where I want and when I hit space it just—it's done. And here, say, "False." So, we've disabled the button by default. And then let's go down to the Changed field and then...

```
private void InitializeComponent()
{

    .

    .

    .

    this.Controls.Add (this.button1);
    this.Controls.Add (this.textBox1);
    this.Controls.Add (this.label1);
    button1.Enabled = false;
}
```

Robert Hess: And actually what you could have done there instead in the design mode, you could have scrolled down to Properties...

Brian Harry: That is correct...

Robert Hess: And set that value to "False" and it would have done the exact same thing.

Brian Harry: And it would have done exactly the same thing.

Brian Harry: So here's my event function that the designer inserted for me when I double clicked on the edit control. So now I need to make it so that as I type, it changes the state of the button. So we'll just very simply say, "button1.Enabled equals"; now I want to look at the TextBox. So it's TextBox1.—and now again, I get this and this time I want to look at the text property, which is the property that always contains the contents of whatever is currently in the TextBox, not equal to empty string. So, basically, that says, "If it's not equal to an empty string, then I want the button enabled. If it is equal to an empty string, then I don't want the button enabled."

```
protected void TextBox1_TextChanged (System.Object sender,...
{
    button1.Enabled = (textBox1.Text != "");
}
```

So, let's just take that and build it. And run it. And you'll see the "Add" button has initially come up disabled, and as I type, it re-enables, and if I delete all the text, it re-disables again. So, from a very simple programming model, very nice integration of the designer with the source code, you can do a lot of things in either one, either using the designer to drag and drop and set properties, or just go into code view and type as you go. And you have so much help as you're going from Visual Studio prompting you, sort of given the context that you're in, what you've typed so far, what the possibilities, the choices you have at this point. And what I showed you here, I didn't actually call any functions that took any significant number of parameters, but it can show you both the member methods and properties, if I type a variable or a class name, and once I've sort of hit open paren on a function for a parameter list, it will then pull up the choices of parameters. Let me just do that, just so you can see it. Let's say like this.Controls. I'll just replicate one of these lines up here, and now I hit the open parens and it's going to tell me both the type, which is a control. It's System.WinForms.Control and the name of the parameter, which is at this point called Value. So this just is a huge productivity advantage. Now it's not new to VB programmers. VB programmers have had this, but it is just a massive—or I should say VB programmers have had this for some controls. VB had a documentation mechanism for doing this kind of thing.

Robert Hess: For that in VB, somebody had to actually take and write some sort of separate file that maintained all of this information separately, whereas you're actually walking into the structure that was written, as it was written, and passing it on.

Brian Harry: In a lot of cases, that is exactly correct.

Robert Hess: Now from a programmer's standpoint, it sounds like this would greatly increase the productivity of programmers, have less chance for getting the wrong function calls, getting the wrong parameters listed, not understanding how to use a particular function, getting a documentation that's one rev back and having to figure out how that relates to the current rev. Do you see that the same level of productivity is going to be equally valuable for both the Web and for the Windows applications on the platforms?

Brian Harry: Absolutely. This same tool provides exactly the same kind of features for whatever application model you're using. Whether you're using the WinForms application model or the Web application model. If I had been doing a Web page instead of a WinForm, it would have felt very much the same. In fact, I would have a form and I could drag and drop controls out of the toolbox. I could set properties. I could double click on a control and it would add an event handler, and I could go and modify that event handler. Again, since the application model is different, some of the API functions I would be calling would be different. And of course what's happening under the covers is very different. There is, however, a large set of things that are completely common across both application models. The whole base class libraries, file IO, data access, net classes, et cetera, are the same, and then we just have these two application models that sit on top of all that and provide a very rich and powerful way to build applications within that application model. But you're not limited to just those two. We talk about those two a lot because they're the kind that lots of people like to build, but you can build command-line console applications including from VB, which is something you didn't used to be able to do particularly easily. You can build NT services including from VB, again something that's not particularly easy.

Robert Hess: And now with using the class libraries, that makes it really easy.

Brian Harry: Yes it does, so we've provided a very general system for building any kind of application you can build today, and they're available to all the languages.

Robert Hess: So, what then, just as closing remarks here, do you think are the most important things for application developers to understand about what the .NET Framework provides them and why it's important to their development moving forward?

Brian Harry: Okay. The .NET Framework is a multi-language environment that provides you a choice of what language you want to use. Its primary goal is about making development easier, faster, more productive, to create the rich applications that you know today, and to do new kinds of applications like Web Services that either can't be done today or at least are very hard to do today. A lot of plumbing has to be written in order to make it possible. Also, to enable safe and secure deployment, we have a bunch of features that eliminate a bunch of the problems we have today with COM components around system instability by when I update software packages and we have globally shared components. And, in addition, we have a security model that enables mobile code, code to be downloaded over the Internet and used without sort of a lot of the virus problems that we have today. So those are probably the key things I'd like people to come away with.

Robert Hess: Well, thank you, Brian. Now, I suppose there's probably going to be some users out there who watched you using Visual Studio and they weren't at the PDC, and they would love to get their hands on something like that. What are their options?

Brian Harry: Well, today the best thing to do is to download the .NET Framework SDK from MSDN.microsoft.com/net, and it has in it everything you need to do everything you saw me do today, except for the design experience part. And we even have a fairly simple designer to enable you to do a lot of that. It's called WinDes. But it includes the VB compiler, the C# compiler and the Managed C++ compiler. It also includes all the libraries that you saw there described in Meteor, and basically everything you need for building ASP+ applications, for building WinForms applications, for building command-lines, et cetera. As far as Visual Studio goes, if you were at the PDC, et cetera, you got that on the CD. If you weren't at the PDC, we've not been distributing that in any other forum. It's going to beta later this fall, and you can sign up for the beta, also I believe on MSDN.microsoft.com.

Robert Hess: Okay, and I'll include a link to that in the bottom of the transcript window that shows people how they can connect up to that.

Brian Harry: Okay.

Robert Hess: Well, thanks a lot, Brian. I appreciate the information you shared with us and I'm sure our audience out there figured out why .NET's important to them.

Brian Harry: Great.

Robert Hess: So thanks for joining us with this episode about the .NET Framework. Hopefully you saw some aspects of why the class libraries and some of the tools coming out really can help you an awful lot in developing your applications. Now in the next episode—we'll come back in about a month from now—we'll be talking about C# specifically, and so that will greatly tie into some of the things we've talked about today. So thanks for joining us and stay tuned for the rest of the show.

For the skills you need on the job.
And on the exam.

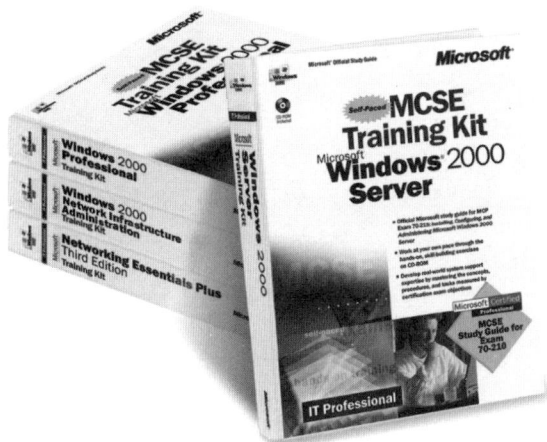

Master the skills tested by the Microsoft Certified Systems Engineer (MCSE) exams—and, more critically, by the job—with official MCSE TRAINING KITS. These book-and-CD self-study kits take you inside Microsoft technologies, teaching you everything you need to know to plan, deploy, and support business-critical systems. Best of all, *you* drive the instruction—working through the lessons and skill-building exercises on your own time, at your own pace. It's learning you can really put to work!

Core Requirements Kit:
U.S.A. $199.99
Canada $289.99

Accelerated Kit:
U.S.A. $89.99
Canada $129.99

All others:
U.S.A. $59.99
Canada $86.99 or $92.99

(see **mspress.microsoft.com/certification** for details)

Windows 2000 Core Requirements

MCSE Training Kit: Microsoft® Windows® 2000 Core Requirements
ISBN 0-7356-1130-0
Four kits in one!

MCSE Training Kit: Microsoft Windows 2000 Server
ISBN 1-57231-903-8

MCSE Training Kit: Microsoft Windows 2000 Professional
ISBN 1-57231-901-1

MCSE Training Kit: Microsoft Windows 2000 Network Infrastructure Administration
ISBN 1-57231-904-6

MCSE Training Kit: Microsoft Windows 2000 Active Directory™ Services
ISBN 0-7356-0999-3

MCSE Training Kit: Microsoft Windows 2000 Accelerated
ISBN 0-7356-1249-8

Core Credits and Electives

MCSE Training Kit: Designing Microsoft Windows 2000 Network Security
ISBN 0-7356-1134-3

MCSE Training Kit: Designing a Microsoft Windows 2000 Network Infrastructure
ISBN 0-7356-1133-5

MCSE Training Kit: Designing a Microsoft Windows 2000 Directory Services Infrastructure
ISBN 0-7356-1132-7

MCSE Training Kit: Migrating from Microsoft Windows NT® 4.0 to Microsoft Windows 2000
ISBN 0-7356-1239-0

Microsoft Press® products are available worldwide wherever quality computer books are sold. For more information, contact your book or computer retailer, software reseller, or local Microsoft® Sales Office, or visit our Web site at mspress.microsoft.com. To locate your nearest source for Microsoft Press products, or to order directly, call 1-800-MSPRESS in the United States (in Canada, call 1-800-268-2222).

Prices and availability dates are subject to change.

Microsoft®
mspress.microsoft.com

For the skills you need on the job.
And on the MCP exam.

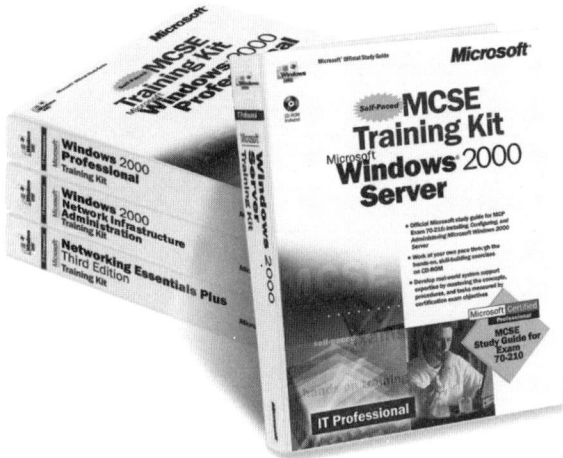

Learn by doing—learn for the job—with official MCSE TRAINING KITS. Whether you choose a book-and-CD Training Kit or the all-multimedia learning experience of an Online Training Kit, you'll gain hands-on experience building essential systems support skills—as you prepare for the corresponding MCP exam. It's official Microsoft self-paced training—how, when, and where you study best.

Windows 2000 Track

MCSE Training Kit, Microsoft® Windows® 2000 Core Requirements
ISBN 0-7356-1130-0

MCSE Training Kit, Microsoft Windows 2000 Server
ISBN 1-57231-903-8

MCSE Online Training Kit, Microsoft Windows 2000 Server
ISBN 0-7356-0954-3
COMING SOON

MCSE Training Kit, Microsoft Windows 2000 Professional
ISBN 1-57231-901-1

MCSE Online Training Kit, Microsoft Windows 2000 Professional
ISBN 0-7356-0953-5
COMING SOON

MCSE Training Kit, Microsoft Windows 2000 Active Directory™ Services
ISBN 0-7356-0999-3

MCSE Training Kit, Microsoft Windows 2000 Network Infrastructure Administration
ISBN 1-57231-904-6

Upgrading to Microsoft Windows 2000 Training Kit
ISBN 0-7356-0940-3

Microsoft SQL Server™ 7.0 System Administration Online Training Kit
ISBN 0-7356-0678-1

Windows NT® 4.0 Track

Microsoft Certified Systems Engineer Core Requirements Training Kit
ISBN 1-57231-905-4

MCSE Training Kit, Networking Essentials Plus, Third Edition
ISBN 1-57231-902-X

MCSE Online Training Kit, Networking Essentials Plus
ISBN 0-7356-0880-6

Electives

Microsoft SQL Server 7.0 Database Implementation Training Kit
ISBN 1-57231-826-0

Microsoft SQL Server 7.0 Database Implementation Online Training Kit
ISBN 0-7356-0679-X

Microsoft SQL Server 7.0 System Administration Training Kit
ISBN 1-57231-827-9

Microsoft®
mspress.microsoft.com